D1196498

THE PAPYRI
OF
ABRAHAM

FACSIMILES OF
THE EVERLASTING
COVENANT

THE PAPYRI
OF
ABRAHAM

FACSIMILES OF
THE EVERLASTING
COVENANT

By Thomas D. Cottle

Artwork Acknowledgments:

Page 32—Egyptian coffins containing mummies
E.A. Wallis Budge, *The Dwellers on the Nile*. 1983
Dover Publications, Inc. Used by permission.

Page 60—Lion couch scenes
E.A. Wallis Budge, *Osiris & the Egyptian Resurrection*, Vol. 2
Dover Publications, Inc. Used by permission.

Page 75—Artwork of the four entities (bottom image)
Franc J. Newcomb & Gladys A Reichard, *Sandpaintings of the Navajo Shooting Chant*. 1975
Dover Publications, Inc. Used by permission.

Page 96—Father Sun, Mother Earth
Franc J. Newcomb & Gladys A Reichard, *Sandpaintings of the Navajo Shooting Chant*. 1975
Dover Publications, Inc. Used by permission.

Page 120—Palette of Narmer
E.A. Wallis Budge, *The Mummy: A Handbook of Egyptian Funerary Archaeology*. 1989
Dover Publications, Inc. Used by permission.

Page 121—Egyptian art of the goddess Hathor
E.A. Wallis Budge, *The Gods of the Egyptians*, Vol 1, 1969 and *The Mummy: A Handbook of Egyptian Funerary Archaeology*. 1989
Dover Publications, Inc. Used by permission.

Page 123—Cow images of the goddess Hathor
E.A. Wallis Budge, *The Gods of the Egyptians*, Vol 1, 1969
Dover Publications, Inc. Used by permission.

Page 141—Coronation and kiosk scenes
E.A. Wallis Budge, *The Gods of the Egyptians*, Vol 2, 1969 and *Osiris & the Egyptian Resurrection*, Vol 1, 1973
Dover Publications, Inc. Used by permission.

Cover and Book Design by Bay Design and Illustration

ISBN 1-889063-05-3

Printed in the United States of America

Published by Insight
Portland, Oregon

This book is dedicated to my wife,
Patricia Carol Cottle

Table of Contents

Acknowledgments

Deep gratitude is expressed to the professionals: Heidi Bay, who designed and typeset the book, Aimee Erickson, who contributed her beautiful artwork, and Paul Rawlins, who edited the manuscript. Their passion for perfection is greatly appreciated.

I express love and thanksgiving for my four sons: Jeff, Mike and Mark for their confidence and help, and Jim who again directed the logistics of the manuscript to publication.

Appreciation is expressed to many professional friends for their valuable suggestions and for having faith that a neophyte layman could make a contribution.

Eternal thanks to Mary Lou who introduced me to Abraham.

Last, but not least, I would like to thank my wife Patti whose love, patience, encouragement, and personal talents made this book possible.

Introduction

"Understanding of added truth enhances abilities in the world today and the eternities of tomorrow."

—Russell M. Nelson

The motivation for publishing this work started many years ago while attending Education Week at Brigham Young University. Dr. Robert J. Matthews, former Dean of Religion at BYU, for whom I have so much respect, made the statement that with so many important religious subjects to be researched and so few to do the work, more saints should become involved. This was fortified by statements such as "We want you to furnish your share to the fund of information, and not cry, all the day long, give, give, give, without imparting anything to the giver"[1] and "The genius of the kingdom with which we are associated is to disseminate knowledge through all the ranks of the people, and to make every man a prophet and every woman a prophetess, that they may understand the plans and purposes of God."[2]

Over the years my personal interests have led me to do research in several categories. This area of interest began with a statement made by Joseph Smith in 1841 just after translating the Book of Abraham and prior to presenting the facsimiles to the Saints. He said,

> Everlasting covenant was made between three personages before the organization of this earth, and relates to their dispensation of things to men on the earth; these personages, according to Abraham's record, are called God the first, the

Creator; God the second, the Redeemer; and God the third,
the witness or Testator.[3]

Notice the prophet Joseph said that this information was according to Abraham's record. The Book of Abraham containing the facsimiles and section 132 in the Doctrine and Covenants are the only
extensive records of or about Abraham that The Church of Jesus
Christ of Latter-day Saints has canonized. Section 132 of the Doctrine & Covenants speaks to all the ingredients of Joseph's statement, but it was modern revelation and not Abraham's record. If
the information that was given to Joseph by Abraham is not in the
chapters of the Book of Abraham, the only other records would be
the facsimiles. Of the three, Facsimile No. 2 seems to fit. The study
began and passion grew.

As research progressed on the facsimiles, it became evident that the
work published on the Egyptian facsimiles was clearly and categor-
ically written with an interpretive approach. The identification of
Egyptian hieroglyphs produced words such as *Ammon, Osiris, Horus,
Canopic figures, crocodile, serpent,* and *baboon.* The leading scholar in
substantiating Abraham and his works was Hugh W. Nibley, with
other contributors being Michael Dennis Rhodes, H. Donl Peterson, Michael Lyon, Jay M. Todd and John Gee, to name a few. Their
contributions on the Book of Abraham and facsimiles have quieted all serious opposition to this theological work.[4] Their accom-
plishments are truly amazing considering they have come from the
comparison of three facsimiles and a few papyri fragments from a
civilization thousands of years old.

Facsimile research into the fruitful prophetic utterances by modern
day prophets and general authorities, along with knowledge from
scriptures and other ancient writings, found vocabulary like Abraham used. Words like: *God, Savior, Holy Ghost, angels, son, daughter,
adversary, priesthood power* and *eternal covenants.* Coupling the ancient
writings, scriptures, and prophetic utterances with the authentic
evidence provided by our LDS scholars has been the foundation of
this work.

The posterity of Abraham is destined to be drawn to his bosom but only as they understand the knowledge he conveyed.[5] This is strongly emphasized in the Book of Mormon concerning

> the covenant people of the Lord; and then shall they know and come to the knowledge of their forefathers, and also to the knowledge of the gospel of their Redeemer, which was ministered unto their fathers by him; wherefore, they shall come to the knowledge of their Redeemer and the very points of his doctrine, that they may know how to come unto him and be saved.[6]

Abraham, the great prophet of his dispensation and father of nations, has passed on to us and all future generations of saints a fuller understanding of these requirements through word and symbol.[7]

The facsimiles of the Book of Abraham have strengthened my personal testimony of eternal covenants. They have increased my testimony of Abraham and Joseph Smith Jr. as prophets of God the Creator, God the Redeemer, and God the Testator. It is hoped that this work will be helpful to those who read it; that testimonies will increase; and like Father Abraham, an appetite, even passion, for more knowledge and greater righteousness will be cultivated. Hopefully, individuals will no longer respond to the facsimiles like a statement made by Shakespeare. "I cannot too much muse such shapes, such gesture, and such sound expression, a kind of excellent dumb discourse."

Chapter 1:
Father Abraham

braham, father of the faithful, could be considered the proto-type for patriarchal fathers. He was outstanding among all the Intelligences, an extremely obedient spirit, and among the most noble and great sons of God. An Old Testament prophet and father of a covenant race, he was a master of theology and astronomy and a pivotal man in the course of world history. During pre-earth life Abraham was a chosen spirit[1] and foreordained to become the head of a great dispensation.[2] His mortal parents were Terah, the eighth great-grandson of Noah, and Amitla (Amalthea), who was probably Terah's second wife.[3] He was named Abram after his mother's father, who died before he was even conceived.[4] *Abram* means "exalted father." The traditional date of his birth is 1996 B.C.[5] This is the date used in the Bible Dictionary and is based on Archbishop Ussher's work; however, there are some doubts regarding Archbishop Ussher's dates.[6] (See Appendix G, "Bible and Civilization Chronology.") There are some who believe Abraham lived much later.

> The age in question, according to Gordon, was the Amarna period, 'the pivotal era of the ancient Near East. In it were blended the civilizations of Mesopotamia, Anotolia, Canaan, Caphor and Egypt.' He thus places Abraham a full six hundred years later than conventional scholars date him."[7]

One interesting clue that may support this claim are the revolution-ary changes that took place in Egypt during the Amarna period, which included the worshiping of one god and a stronger emphasis on family relations. This was the period of Akhenaten, the Pharaoh who abandoned the old gods of Egypt and turned to one god with his wife Nefertiti and their son Tutankhamun. Could these changes have come as a result of Abraham's stay in the land of Egypt?

Other inconsistencies include the location of Abram's childhood home, periods of residency, travel routes, and the sequences of priesthood keys, powers, and blessings he received. This is because the accounts of various events in Abram's life, although numerous, are varied and full of discrepancies. For instance, the Bible iden-tifies "Ur of the Chaldees as the birthplace of Haran but as the birthplace of Abraham, it can only be presumed."[8] The apocryphal[9] Book of Jasher states that Abram's birth was during the cruel reign of Nimrod and that Abram was hid from society by his mother until he was ten years of age[10] at which time he "went to Noah and his son Shem, and he remained with them to learn the instruction of the Lord and his ways" for thirty-nine years. It further tells us that in his fiftieth year he left Noah and Shem and came to his father's house.[11]

Abraham opens his book with the statement, "In the land of the Chaldeans, at the residence of my father, I, Abraham, saw that it was needful for me to obtain another place of residence." This statement could indicate that he had not been at his father's home very long. Abraham then makes it clear that he was a "follower of righteous-ness" and desired "also to be one who possessed great knowledge," which would seem to indicate that he had a strong foundation in the gospel. Certainly, if he had dwelt with Noah and Shem, he would have had this training. Abraham said the Lord told him, "As it was with Noah so shall it be with thee." This seems to infer that he knew a great deal about Noah. Abraham could have been seventy-eight years old when Noah died.[12] The pseudepigraphal[13] Book of Jubilees states that "in the sixtieth year of the life of Abram … Abram arose in the night and burned the house of idols."[14] If, as

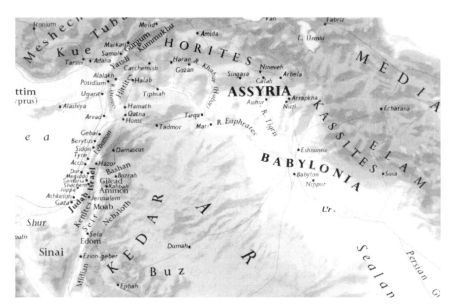

Map of Middle East

Abraham said, he "was sixty and two years old when he departed out of Haran," Jasher's account of Abram's being fifty at the time he came to his father's house could be valid. Abram would then have lived in the land of Ur for over ten years, received heavenly communication about future blessings, married, obtained the Urim and Thummim, received subsequent priesthood authority, survived the sacrificial experience, and burned the idols, all before leaving the land of Chaldees and going to Haran.

While we know that marvelous things happened while Abram was in the land of Ur of Chaldea[15] on the Plain of Olishem,[16] we do not know exactly where Ur was. Some believe its location to be the famous ziggurat-temple of Ur-Nammu which can be seen at Tell al-Magayyar, 150 miles from the Persian Gulf near the lower Euphrates River.[17] Others believe Abraham's Ur was in northern Iraq near the present cities of Harran, Urfa, or Edessa. (See Map of Middle East.) For a scholarly discourse on the location of Ur see Dr. Hugh Nibley's "A New Look at the Pearl of Great Price."[18] The land of Ur must have been a well-developed cultural area with both economic and agricultural abundance. Certainly the Plain of

Olishem would have had a large grazing area to sustain Abraham's herds and flocks, his father's many herds of various kinds, and those of their kinfolk. In addition, the physical conditions of the plains would make the view of the heavens so available that one could see clearly from horizon to horizon.

In Ur, Abraham's father, brothers, and their families were idol worshipers.[19] They had all "turned from righteousness," broken the commandments, and "worshiped gods of the heathen" made "of wood or of stone." In every respect "they [had] turned their hearts away from [the Lord]."[20] Yet their sinful actions went far beyond this. They had their "hearts set to do evil" and were involved in human sacrifice in the "manner of the Egyptian."[21] We learn through Abraham that Egyptian culture was predominant in the land of Ur, as was the worship of the gods of Elkenah, Libnah, Mahmackrah, Korash, and the god of Pharaoh, king of Egypt. An altar in the form of a bedstead and Egyptian hieroglyphics, called Rahleenos by the Chaldeans, were also present.[22]

Although Abram was exposed to the environment of idolatry here, his testimony of Jehovah did not waver. His heart remained pure. In fact, Abraham said that he "sought for the blessings of the fathers" and "to be a father of many nations" and that he "sought for mine appointment unto the priesthood according to the appointment of God unto the fathers concerning the seed."[23] These righteous desires were eventually answered with great blessings and heavenly manifestations. When the priests of Pharaoh sought Abraham's life (exemplified in Facsimile No. 1), he lifted up his voice unto the Lord, "and the Lord hearkened and heard, and he filled me with the vision of the Almighty, and the angel of his presence stood by me, and immediately unloosed my bands."[24] This manifestation of the Godhead braced Abraham's testimony of its three members. Jehovah spoke of the patriarchal order of the priesthood as additional power yet to be bestowed upon Abraham: "Behold, I will lead thee by my hand, and I will take thee, to put upon thee my name, even the Priesthood of thy father, and my power shall be over thee."[25]

It was also at Ur that Abram received the Urim and Thummim, the sacred instrument of translation. *Urim* in Hebrew means "prophecies" or "revelations." *Thummim* in Babylonian means "to speak," "to swear," and the "records of the fathers." The LDS Bible Dictionary says *Urim and Thummim* is a "Hebrew term that means Lights and Perfections." A prophet who had this divine instrument could be in possession of knowledge of all things pertaining to heaven and earth.[26]

With the use of this divine instrument and the information contained in records, Abram acquired additional knowledge concerning "the right of Priesthood," "the plan of creation," and the actual creation itself,[27] "the planets, and the stars,"[28] and the known universe. In addition to the knowledge gleaned from the records and interpreters, the revelations he received expanded his understanding of mathematics and astronomy until it probably equaled or surpassed that of other famous mathematicians and astronomers. Along with the Urim and Thummim came the power of seer as well as the mantle of revelator and prophet.[29] It is interesting to note that these same blessings and powers were bestowed upon Joseph Smith during the early part of his ministry.[30] Joseph must have had the same insight as Abraham when he wrote, "All thrones and dominions, principalities and powers, shall be revealed and set forth upon all who have endured valiantly for the gospel of Jesus Christ," and "if there be bounds set to the heavens or to the seas, or to the dry land, or to the sun, moon, or stars—all the times of their revolutions, all the appointed days, months, and years, and all their glories, laws, and set times, shall be revealed in the days of the dispensation of the fulness of times—according to that which was ordained in the midst of the Council of the Eternal God of all other gods before this world was."[31] (See Appendix B for an outline comparing the lives of Abraham and Joseph Smith.)

Abraham taught that each son and daughter of God was foreordained in the spirit world through the law of election.[32] In mortality, every individual may progress to the full measure of election as they receive the ordinances and covenants set forth in the plan of salvation. Joseph Smith said, "If a man gets a fullness of the priesthood of God, he has to get it in the same way that Jesus Christ obtained it, and that was by keeping all the commandments and obeying all the ordinances of the house of the Lord."[33]

After baptism, the first priesthood Abram would have received was the Holy Priesthood after the Order of the Son of God, known today as the Melchizedek Priesthood. We know from the Doctrine and Covenants that it was Melchizedek who gave this priesthood to Abram, but it seems to have been Shem that he may have lived with according to some accounts. Are Melchizedek and Shem the same person? (See Appendix A, "Melchizedek and Shem.") If Melchizedek was Shem, the son of Noah, it would put everything into its proper perspective. It would answer why it was during Melchizedek's time that the name of the priesthood was changed from "the Holy Priesthood, after the Order of the Son of God" to "the priesthood of Melchizedek."[34] It would certainly explain why Abraham went to so much effort to seek out Melchizedek, who was the "King of Righteousness," "the great High Priest,"[35] and "oldest living patriarch." It would help explain why it was Melchizedek with two counselors that visited Abraham at his encampment at Mamre.[36] It would also explain why Abram was taught about Jesus Christ by Melchizedek, who was a prototype of Christ.[37]

It is not known if or how often Abraham saw Noah, but it appears he was with his son, whether by the name of Shem or Melchizedek, on numerous occasions. It is recorded that Shem was translated either one year or twenty-five years before Abraham died, depending on which dates are used.[38] It is known that Abraham and the great high priest spent much time together. Abram was ordained by Melchizedek and taught by him. The Bible gives an account of their having the sacrament together.[39] Joseph Smith relates to us what Abraham said to Melchizedek: "I believe all that thou hast taught me concerning the priesthood and the coming of the Son of Man; so Melchizedek ordained Abraham and sent him away. Abraham rejoiced, saying, Now I have a priesthood."[40]

After receiving the Melchizedek Priesthood, Abram received additional keys, following the sequence used in other dispensations. If Abram was with Noah and Shem at an early age, he would most likely have received the priesthood as a young man. Noah received it at age ten.[41] The ordination to the Melchizedek Priesthood gave Abram the foundation needed to become a high priest.[42] We know Abraham received additional authority while at Ur, for he said, "In the land of the Chaldeans, at the residence of my fathers…I became a rightful heir, a High Priest, holding the right belonging to the fathers."[43] We learn from the Book of Mormon that Melchizedek was out over all the land preaching repentance and doing missionary work.[44] It is possible that he could have been as far north as Abram's home, where additional priesthood keys of authority would have been given as circumstances warranted. All of this is summarized in the Joseph Smith Translation: "And it came to pass, that God blessed Abram, and gave unto him riches, and honor, and lands for an everlasting possession; according to the covenant which he had made, and according to the blessing wherewith Melchizedek had blessed him."[45] With these powers in place, future ordinations of patriarch, king, and high priest to God were still to come.

In his own account, Abraham tells of his marriage to Sarai while he "was in Ur, in Chaldea.[46] "I, Abraham, took Sarai to wife, and Nahor, my brother, took Milcah [Sarai's sister] to wife, who was the daughter of Haran."[47] Sarai and Abram's marriage would not have been an eternal marriage at this time, for they were among idol worshippers. This eternal ordinance would have occurred after they were endowed with knowledge but before they had children. The name *Sarai* is a derivative of *Sarah*, which means "princess." If Abram was in his forties when he wed, Sarai was in her thirties, for she was ten years younger than her husband.[48] Sarai's mother was Nahariath,[49] who married Sarai's father-in-law, Terah, following the death of her husband Haran. Thus, according to Jewish law, this would make Sarai a daughter (instead of granddaughter) to Terah and a half-sister to Abraham.

As Abram's eternal companion, Sarai, an elect lady, suffered her own trials and tribulations. Her experiences match those of her husband in severity and even exceed them at times.[50] According to all historical accounts, Sarai was an extremely beautiful woman. The Book of Jasher informs us, "And when the officers of the king beheld Sarai they were struck with admiration at the beauty, and all the princes and servants of Pharaoh assembled to see Sarai, for she was very beautiful."[51] Flavius Josephus said, "For the fame of his wife's beauty, was greatly talked of; for which reason Pharaoh, the king of Egypt, would not be satisfied with what was reported of her, but would needs see her himself."[52] A very lovely and vivid description of Sarai (Sarah) comes from the Dead Sea Scrolls, found in the "Memoirs of the Patriarchs." After relating the arrival of Abram and Sarai in the land of Egypt, and after Abram had been warned in a dream, it was written, "Then Sarai [and I journeyed on] towards Zoan ... [but all the while I was] fearful for her lest anyone should set eyes on her. After five years, three Egyptian dignitaries of the Pharaoh of Zoan [confronted me] and my wife." After lavishing great compliments upon Sarai, "they went to present themselves to their master ... reaching the palace they reported to him ... [and] ... began to expatiate on the beauties of Sarai ... How beautiful her eyes! How delicate is her nose and the whole lustre of her countenance! How fair are her breasts ... how perfect her hands! ... how lovely her palms, how long and slender all her fingers! How well-rounded her thighs! No maiden or new-wed bride is fairer than she! Her beauty is greater than all other women's, and she excels them all! What is more, along with all this beauty she has great wisdom, and what-ever she does turns out well."[53] Even God recognized this attribute and told Abraham, "In all that Sarah hath said unto thee, hearken unto her voice."[54] Abraham must have been absolutely captivated by her beauty and wisdom.

Her beauty, however, brought two major trials: one in Egypt with the Pharaoh and the other with Abimelech, king of Gerar.[55] In both of these incidences, the men desired to take Sarai to wife, believing she was Abram's sister. The Lord protected her in both instances. Concerning the Pharaoh, the Book of Jasher says that "when the king came near to Sarai, the angel smote him to the ground, and acted thus to him the whole night, and the king was terrified."[56] Concerning Abimelech, "And he dreamed that an angel of the Lord came to him with a drawn sword in his hand, and the angel stood over Abimelech, and wished to slay him with the sword, and the king was terrified in his dream."[57] It is interesting that Abram later blessed both of these kings, blessings which not only demonstrated that Abram used his priesthood, but clearly illustrated the proper procedure of the "laying on of hands."[58] The blessing given to King Abimelech of Gerar particularly illustrated the true charity within the bowels of Abram. In this blessing, Abram included the king's wife and maidservants. The blessing was fulfilled when children were born to them.[59]

When the Lord gave the commandment to leave Ur, Abram and Sarai began preparations to relocate. The family of Lot, son of Haran, traveled with them.[60] Much was learned from the first full-scale move of this small community of families. Abraham gives a firsthand account of the location and details of each place they stopped as they traveled south towards Egypt. Their first stop was in an area near the source of the Euphrates River. The place was named Haran (Harron, Carrhae, called Charran in the New Testament) after Abraham's deceased brother.

It was in Haran that Abram and Lot prayed to the Lord to turn away the famine from Terah's house that they might not perish, and the Lord appeared unto Abram for the second recorded time. Abram was told that Jehovah would "make of thee a minister to bear my name"[61] and records that the great "I Am" said: "My name is Jehovah, and I know the end from the beginning; therefore my hand shall be over thee."[62] With the famine being abated somewhat, Terah, during a brief period of repentance, took his family and followed his son to Haran, but after his arrival, he turned to his idolatry again.

Abram and Lot had great success with their missionary work in Haran, for when they left this area, they took all "that [they] had gathered, and the souls that [they] had won in Haran, and came forth."[63] This would suggest that the adoption process of the righteous as Abraham's seed may have started here. Concerning this adoption, Jehovah said, "And I will bless them through thy name; for as many as receive this Gospel shall be called after thy name, and shall be accounted thy seed," and "all the families of the earth [shall] be blessed, even with the blessings of the Gospel, which are the blessings of salvation, even of life eternal."[64] It was here at Haran that Abram was informed of additional keys and blessings of the priesthood that were in store for him and his posterity.[65]

Again, in obedience to the call given by Jehovah to travel to Egypt, Abram, Sarai, Lot and his wife, along with their possessions and the converts they had won, left Haran by way of Jershon and traveled south in caravan. Abraham's account of the journey begins with, "But I, Abraham, and Lot, my brother's son, prayed unto the Lord, and the Lord appeared unto me, and said unto me: Arise, and take Lot with thee; for I have purposed to take thee away out of Haran, and to make of thee a minister to bear my name in a strange land which I will give unto thy seed after thee for an everlasting possession, when they hearken to my voice."[66] Concerning the route south, it has been suggested that "there is a possibility that Abram traveled southward on the ancient route by way of Damascus to the site of ancient Jerash (Jershon)."[67] (See map "The Land of Canaan.") Leaving the good life, they became nomads, living in tents, using goats skins in the winter and sackcloth against the heat of the summer, as dependent on their animals as the beasts were on them. From Jershon, their travel would have taken them down the Jabbok River to the Jordan Valley, and upon reaching the river, they most likely crossed at the ancient city of Adam.[68] From there they would have traveled up the broad Wadi Farah (Faria) to Tirzah, one of the ancient capitols of Israel.[69] Here they faced the steep ascent of Wadi Beidon onto the plateau of Shechem to the city Sichem[70] (Shechem, Sechem, or Sychem). This was the shortest route from the Jordan Valley to Shechem.

Shechem, now modern Nablus, is one of the most ancient towns of Palestine and is situated on a beautiful plain among the moun-

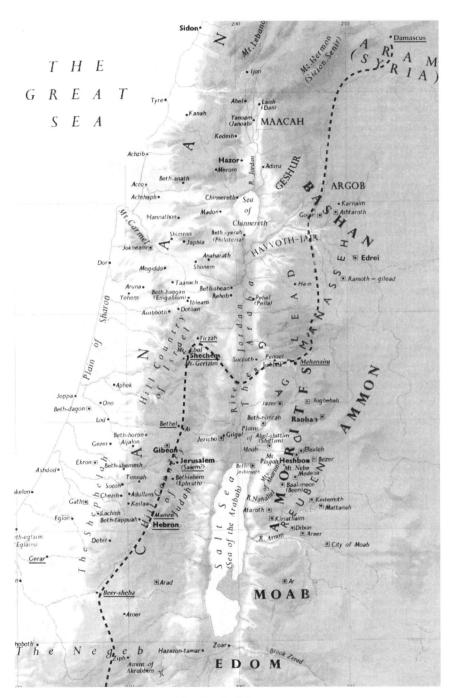

The Land of Canaan

tains of Ephraim between the hills Ebal and Gerizim. Abraham's campsite would have been on the Plain of Moreh, where he built the second altar on the journey and offered sacrifice as he asked for protection while in "this idolatrous nation": "And the Lord appeared unto me in answer to my prayers, and said unto me: Unto thy seed will I give this land."[71] Shechem later became one of the seven Levite cities of refuge. The bones of Joseph, Abraham's great-grandson, were eventually buried here.

Moving south, the travelers pitched their tents between Bethel and Ai, an area made up of steep, rocky, dry, brown and black forbidding hills and valleys. Upon arriving here Abram went up on the mountain and built an altar. He declared unto the Lord, "You (are) my God, the eternal God."[72] According to the Old Testament, an altar on a mountain is often equivalent to a temple of the Lord. It is interesting that in both Abraham's account and in the Apocrypha, there is no mention of any response to Abram's petitions. This would be consistent with not revealing sacred experiences connected with a temple of God. Bethel ("House of God"), formerly called Luz and now Beltin, is one of the most sacred spots in Israel. It was Jacob, Abraham's grandson, who had a dream at Bethel, set up a pillar, and named the town. Bethel later became significant to both the future prophet Samuel and King Jeroboam. Biblical, apocryphal, and Abraham's personal accounts of the journey south end at Bethel. None of the records mention Hebron, even though the families traveled the southern route to Hebron–Mamre, which passes right by Jerusalem (Salem), home of Shem-Melchizedek.

With famine again so prevalent, and knowing Egypt to be a land of plenty, Abram and Sarai made the decision to go there.[73] The Lord instructed Abraham at this point to tell all foreigners that Sarai was his sister.[74] He was also reminded of his errand in going to Egypt: "And the Lord said unto me: Abraham, I show these things unto thee before ye go into Egypt, that ye may declare all these words."[75]

Abram and his caravan traveled from Bealoth south to Egypt, probably along the route to the Red Sea. The first Pharaoh of Egypt was blessed by Noah, Abraham's great-grandfather, "with the blessings of the earth, and with the blessings of wisdom, but cursed ... as pertaining to the Priesthood," for "Pharaoh being of that lineage by which he could not have the right of Priesthood, notwithstanding the Pharaohs would fain claim it from Noah, through Ham."[76] Historically, Egypt has always been tied economically to Canaan by both land travel and sea. The caravan routes across Sinai took about a week of desert travel, while the ships that plied the sea route were much quicker, running directly along the coast of Canaan, passing Joppa, Tyre, Sidon, and Gebal. The Pharaohs had strong footholds in both Palestine and Syria during the Twelfth Dynasty of the Middle Kingdom (ca. 1991–ca. 1786 B.C.). Thus, as Abraham relates, the Israelites and their families had many experiences with Egyptians.

The Dead Sea Scrolls reveal of this period that

> a famine swept the entire country. Hearing that there was produce in Egypt, I made my way ... that is, to the land of Egypt. Eventually I reached the C-r-m-o-n, one of the arms of the river (of Egypt) ... and leaving our own land behind, entered the land of Egypt, which belonged to the children of Ham.

The Book of Jubilees says they went "into Egypt in the third year and he stayed in Egypt five years before his wife was taken from him."[77] (Additional information concerning Egypt can be found in A Genesis Apocryphon column XIX, 9–27 14–21 & column XX, 2–34; the Book of Jasher, chapter XV. 1–33; and the Apocalypse of Abraham 22:1–5.)

In the third chapter of Abraham, the Lord instructs Abram to teach astronomy and gospel truths in Egypt. It is enlightening to observe how these two subjects form a dualism and can be overlaid with each other by the "also" in verse eighteen. "Star" can be substituted for "spirit" and visa versa, illustrating that the doctrine Abraham presents in this chapter applies to all of God's creations. Flavius

Josephus discussed these two subjects but reversed the order of them. He placed theology as the first assignment of Abraham's divine decree. Josephus tells us that

> Abram had discovered that the Egyptians were in a flourishing condition, he [Abraham] was disposed to go down to them, both to partake of the plenty they enjoyed and to become an auditor of their priests, and to know what they said concerning the gods ... to convert them to a better way.

Only after this comment does Josephus mention astronomy. "He communicated ... and delivered to them the science of astronomy; for, before Abram came into Egypt, they were unacquainted with those parts of learning."[78] The Egyptians certainly did not need knowledge of the heavens for navigation or direction. Ninety-five percent of the population lived on the Nile River, which flows from south to north. Every Egyptian knew the direction of north by looking at the water flow. The knowledge they needed was that of gospel truths, and the principles of astronomy could be used to teach them about God and the creations. The Egyptian royalty, as well as the priests of Egypt, were conversant with astronomy, the wonders of which are evidenced by the Egyptians' remarkable construction. What they needed to understand, however, was that the center of the Egyptian heavens was not the only center. Abraham's errand was to teach that God was the true center of the heavens and the source of all powers and blessings.

Concerning the historical period of Abram's sojourn in Egypt, we know that Abram and Sarai visited the court of Pharaoh. The Pharaoh was a descendant of Ham through his fourth son, Canaan,[79] during this Middle Kingdom of Egyptian history. At this time, the Pharaoh's court was chiefly from the Memphis and Fayum districts. It was during this time that Abram became a mighty prince and received unimaginable blessings. Where Abram lived exactly is not known. It was possibly the great cultural center of Tanis, the capitol of Egypt for 350 years, but to date, the location of this city has not been found.[80] The period and places during Abram and Sarai's stay in Egypt seem entirely speculative.

We do know that while in Egypt, Abram and Sarai did all that they were commanded to do. It appears that no ordinations or keys were bestowed upon Abram while he was in Egypt, as all priesthood keys were in Canaan with priesthood leadership. Abram did learn a great deal about Egyptian conceptions of truth, justice, and righteousness and became widely known and esteemed because of his great contributions of wisdom and knowledge. In gratitude, Pharaoh bestowed upon Abraham great wealth and material possessions when Abraham left Egypt. We have no firsthand information in the Book of Abraham concerning his departure from Egypt because Abraham did not write about it. Information available on this subject is in the Bible and Apocrypha, and we are blessed to have the corrections and additions made by Joseph Smith in his translation of the Old Testament. The Bible tells us that Abraham "had sheep, and oxen, and he asses, and menservants, and maidservants, and she asses, and camels."[81] With all of these great herds and material possessions, the exit northward out of Egypt would have been considerably slower and more cumbersome than their entry. The desire to travel great distances may have been somewhat diminished. Their departure would certainly have required careful preparation. Their route out of Egypt is unknown.

We do know that the first recorded destination of Abram is the barren, rocky mountain altar at Bethel (which is to the north), where Abram and Lot offered up their gratitude for the blessings of protection and safekeeping they received in Egypt. Certainly they would have stopped at other locations, for they were a much larger caravan of people, animals, and possessions than they had been on their journey south. Even Lot had a heavy stock of cattle, flocks and herds, and tents. To reach Bethel, they would have passed Hebron-Mamre and Jerusalem. Why did they go the extra distance? Why did they go past Mamre, where so many spiritual blessings were to take place, and past Melchizedek's home? Why is nothing recorded about these earlier locations?[82] Was the altar on the mountain at Bethel their temple? Its being the first place mentioned on the journey out of Egypt may again indicate the sacredness of this location. It also raises the possibility that Abraham and Lot went on

Mosque of Abraham

alone, leaving the great herds south of Jerusalem where the "grazing-ground" was more abundant. This would seem consistent with the narratives of herdsmen quarreling and Lot's leaving and going to Sodom.

In any event, we are told about Abraham's leaving Bethel. "Then Abram removed his tent, and came and dwelt in the plain of Mamre, which is in Hebron, and built there an altar unto the Lord"[83] and "remained in that place many years."[84] Hebron (Kirjoth-Arba) is twenty miles south of Jerusalem. At 3,040 feet above the Mediterranean Sea, it is the highest town in Israel. Located in the Negev dryland, it fell along the main line of travel through the Judean hill country. It was in this place that Abraham purchased a plot of ground with a cave to be used as a family cemetery. Later, it became the burial ground for Abraham and Sarah, Isaac and Rebekah, Jacob and Leah, and others of their family. King Herod ordered a compound to be built over the cave of Machpelah, and although it was started, it was not completed until the Byzantine and Crusader times and was called "The Tomb of the Patriarchs." It is now called "The Mosque of Abraham," for Hebron today is occupied predominantly by Muslims. This area is holy to all three monotheistic religions which claim Abraham as their father. It is interesting that this building has been used both as a Jewish synagogue and Muslim mosque. (See photo of the "Mosque of Abraham.") Later, before King David united the country, Hebron became the capitol of Judah.

We also get some indication of Abraham's age at or near this time. It is recorded in the "Memoirs of the Patriarchs" in the Dead Sea Scrolls that "God appeared to Abram in a vision and said to him: 'Behold, it is ten full years since you were up from Haran. Two years have you passed here, and seven in Egypt, and one since

you came back from Egypt."[85]
It seems plausible that Abram
was seventy-five years old
when he returned to Hebron.
By Abraham's own record
he was sixty-two when he
left Haran. By adding ten
years to sixty-two we are in
harmony.[86]

Egyptian circumcision scene

Here at Hebron, Abram was
again visited by Jehovah and
received many great blessings. There are indications that it may have
been here where the Lord gave Abram and Sarai their endowment
and sealing. Certainly Abram and Sarai had demonstrated a form
of perfection regarding their errand in Egypt, where Abram and
Sarai accomplished all that they were asked to do. Their faith was
measured and found sufficient. Their names were subsequently
changed to Abraham and Sarah, and they received an endowment
of power.[87] Jehovah declared the covenant that would "make of
thee a great nation, and I will bless thee, and make thy name great;
and thou shalt be a blessing."[88] God also promised Abram that
he would receive an inheritance of land and "blessings of great
measure," hear the declaration of Jehovah, have seed as numerous as
the sands, and, finally, that he could know that the rights and powers
of the priesthood "shall continue in thee" forever. It was at this time
that the Lord made another covenant with Abraham, as he had with
Noah, in the form of an ordinance.[89] Following this ordinance and
the making of the covenant, the Lord said, "Walk before me, and
be thou perfect."[90] The Joseph Smith Translation tells us that the
covenant of circumcision was introduced at this time to establish a
token of the everlasting covenant between Abraham and the Lord.

> And I will establish a covenant of circumcision with thee, and it
> shall be my covenant between me and thee, and thy seed after thee,
> in their generations; that thou mayest know for ever that children
> are not accountable before me until they are eight years old.[91]

This token of the covenant had great significance and was instigated along with all requirements given by the Lord at this time.
(See the "Egyptian circumcision scene.")

After receiving this endowment, Abraham could now receive the
keys of the sealing power of the Melchizedek Priesthood which
the fathers had possessed and which Abraham had so long desired.
These ordinances most likely took place when Abraham paid his
tithes to the great high priest Melchizedek. The Joseph Smith
Translation says, "And this Melchizedek, having thus established
righteousness, was called the king of heaven by his people, or in
other words, the king of peace. And he lifted up his voice, and he
blessed Abram." Truly, this was one of the most significant events
of biblical times. The apostle Paul said, "For this Melchisedec, king
of Salem, priest of the most high God, who met Abraham return-
ing from the slaughter of the kings, and blessed him; To whom also
Abraham gave a tenth part of all."[92] The Book of Jasher says, "And
Adonizedek king of Salem, the same was Shem, went out with his
men to meet Abram ... and Adonizedek blessed Abram, and Abram
gave him a tenth from all."[93]

The further authority or key given at this time was described by
Joseph Smith. After Abraham gave Melchizedek "a tenth part of
all his spoils," he then "received a blessing under the hands of
Melchizedek even the last law or a fulness of the law or priesthood
which constituted him a king and priest ... or an endless life"[94]
The preparation for this fullness of the law would have been the
sealing authority for his posterity and the patriarchal order of the
Melchizedek Priesthood, which provides the authority for eternal
marriage and eternal seed, or posterity. The patriarchal order of
the Melchizedek Priesthood and sealing keys that had come down
from Adam were now in place for Abraham and his posterity. This
would have fulfilled the declaration that "after the days of Noah an
order was introduced called the patriarchal order, in which every
man managed his own family affairs, and prominent men among
them ... officiated in what is known among us as the Priesthood
of the Son of God."[95] Modern revelation shows that these blessings

are similar to those Joseph and Emma received—the same blessings which are available to every eternal unit of Abraham's posterity. They "shall inherit thrones, kingdoms, principalities, and powers, dominions, all heights and depths."[96]

Abraham was now a high priest of God after the holy order. "A high priest holding the right belonging to the ... fathers" refers to the patriarchal order of the priesthood and is much different from a high priest within the Melchizedek Priesthood.[97] Up until now the Lord had compared Abraham's seed to the finite dust of the earth. From this point on, he compared Abraham's seed to the infinite stars of heaven. "Look now towards heaven, and tell the stars, if thou be able to number them: and he said unto him, So shall thy seed be."[98] With these blessings comes the knowledge of kings and priests, queens and priestesses.[99] This was truly a fulfillment of the higher blessings Abraham desired when he had "sought for ... the right whereunto I should be ordained to administer the same."[100] Abraham was also privileged to see in vision the days of the ministry of the Son of Man, Jehovah's mortal sojourn as Jesus Christ.[101] As they progressed along their spiritual journey, Abraham and Sarah now awaited the visitation of the comforters.[102]

Abraham is called "father" in the same context that Adam is called father. *Father* is synonymous with *patriarch*: "Adam was the natural father of his posterity ... over whom he presided as Patriarch, Prophet, Priest, and King. Both Abraham and Jacob stood in the same relationship to their families."[103] Abraham personally blessed not only his son Isaac but also his immediate family, through whom the blessing flowed to all his righteous descendants.[104] Abraham's dispensation was the last to hold the "patriarchal order" of the Melchizedek Priesthood with its sacred keys, power, and ordinances,[105] and Abraham, his son Isaac, and his grandson Jacob were the last of the patriarchs to minister to their own families through this authority. To each of these three patriarchs, the great I Am gave the same authority and entered into the same eternal covenant, hence the well-known declaration, "Jehovah, God of

Abraham, Isaac, and Jacob." In our dispensation, Joseph Smith was not at first a prophet-father in the same capacity as Abraham or Adam. It was not "Father" but "Brother Joseph" and "Brother Brigham," for they were prophets to the world and became patriarchs, fathers to their seed, only after they received the ordinance of celestial marriage and covenanted to preside over an eternal family as the patriarch-father. Biblical fathers with the patriarchal order of the priesthood brought gospel blessings first to their family and then to the gentile posterity of Adam and Eve.[106] Abraham said that through this order of the priesthood "shall all the families of the earth be blessed, even with the blessings of the gospel, which are the blessings of salvation, even of life eternal."[107]

Today the blessings of the patriarchal order of the priesthood come by way of eternal marriage, the type of marriage Adam and Eve received when they were married by God.[108] We learn the following from Nephi in the Book of Mormon:

> Wherefore, our father hath not spoken of our seed alone, but also of all the house of Israel, pointing to the covenant which should be fulfilled in the latter days; which covenant the Lord made to our father Abraham, saying: In thy seed shall all the kindred of the earth be blessed.[109]

This is a fulfillment of the Lord's promise given to Abraham while he was at Haran. The keys of priesthood authority needed to accomplish this come to the prophet of each new dispensation sequentially as the Saints of that dispensation are prepared to receive them.[110] These keys and authority are the means by which the head of the dispensation can do the work, bring glory to the Father, and accomplish his primary errand from the Father, which is to teach Jesus Christ and him crucified. Once the authority is in place, every power and blessing the keys provide becomes available to every faithful member who enters into the covenant, either in mortality or in the spirit world.

The timing involved in restoring the keys is different in each dispensation, but the sequence is the same. Adam's was the longest period, when he lived close to one thousand years, while Joseph Smith's was the shortest, as he lived only thirty-eight years. The pattern can be determined by reviewing when the keys were given to each prophet in their dispensation. Our own dispensation of the fullness of times has specific and complete records of this process.[111] Remember, Joseph Smith was first called to be a seer, translator, prophet, apostle, and elder by virtue of his ordinations. Seven years later, further priesthood keys were restored at the Kirtland Temple. Later he was married for time and all eternity, and after all priesthood orders were his, Joseph said, ten months before his martyrdom, "there are three grand orders of priesthood referred to here. 1st The King of Shiloam (Melchizedek) had power and authority over that of Abraham, holding the key and the power of endless life."[112] Joseph had at this time the fullness of the priesthood of the Son of God with all three grand orders, Melchizedek, Patriarchal, and Aaronic.

For Abraham and Sarah, blessings of the fullness of the priesthood were still to come. We may ask, what is meant by the fullness of the priesthood? Daniel Tyler, a mission president to Italy and survivor of the Martin Handcart Company, writing for the *Juvenile Instructor*, said,

> It does not mean any special office ... but there were powers belonging to the different grades of priesthood ... men may be ordained to other grades of priesthood without obtaining a fullness thereof. The Lord informed the prophet (Joseph Smith) that the temples were the place to receive 'the fullness of the priesthood.' These additional powers include all of the keys that belong to the holy priesthood on the earth or were ever revealed to man in any dispensation.[113]

This may be the very reason our dispensation is called the "Dispensation of the Fulness of Times." As beautifully revealed and recorded in the twenty-first verse of section 128 in the Doctrine and Covenants, every key, honor, majesty, glory, and power from all other dispensations has been restored to our day and time. The President of The Church of Jesus Christ of Latter-day Saints is in possession of every key from all previous periods of the Lord's church, including the time of Adam and Eve. As a church, every worthy covenanted son and daughter in every country on the entire earth can rest assured that the potential of all that Brother Tyler has spoken of is available to them. All of which equates to the "Perfecting of the Saints."

As Abraham and Sarah continued in their quest to receive all blessings the Lord promises to the faithful, Sarah obeyed the commandment given to Abraham to take Hagar to wife, thereby implementing the law of plural marriage. When Hagar bore Ishmael, the "Law of Sarah" was instigated in their dispensation. "And why did she [Sarah] do it? Because this was the law"[114] implemented to fulfill the promises made to Abraham in relationship to the blessings his seed would bring to the posterity of Adam and Eve. Father Abraham had been guaranteed that the posterity of the gentile, or non-Israelite, lineage could be adopted and become "heirs according to the promise" of the seed of Abraham.[115] The eventual outcome would be all of his posterity, which would be as numerous as the stars of heaven and sands of the seashore[116] sitting "down with Abraham, and Isaac, and Jacob, in the kingdom of heaven."[117] Joseph Smith taught that after faith, repentance and baptism, the "effect of the Holy Ghost upon a Gentile is to purge out the old blood, and make him actually of the seed of Abraham. That man that has none of the blood of Abraham (naturally) must become a new creation through the ordinances of the everlasting covenant."[118]

After their stay in Hebron, Abraham and Sarah moved to Gerar, which was located southeast of Gaza on elevated pastureland and which was the land of the Philistines. It was the king of Gerar whom Abraham went to see for permission to settle Beersheba. Abraham and Sarah had the same experience with Abimelech, king of Gerar, that they had with Pharaoh while in Egypt.[119] After obtaining the king's permission they moved to Beersheba. This area was blessed with the rich pastureland needed for their numerous herds and flocks. Beersheba ("Well of the Oath") became the home of Abraham. It was given this name because of the covenant Abraham made here with Abimelech. The location of Beersheba is close to the middle of the thirty-mile Negeb dryland. "In the Bible, Negev is translated 'south' or 'southland.' The passage, 'Abram journeyed, going on still toward the south,' reads 'toward the Negev' in the Hebrew text."[120] At Beersheba Abraham again built an altar and called on "the everlasting God."[121] Three men appear, and the great declaration that Sarah will have a son is given.[122] Thirteen years later, in Negeb on the Plains of Mamre, Sarah would bear Isaac, the promised son, whose name means "He laugheth."

The episode of God commanding Abraham to sacrifice Isaac in the land of Moriah "upon one of the mountains which I will tell thee of"[123] has probably been told more than any other story in the Old Testament. It was known in the Americas five hundred years before Christ:

> Behold, they believed in Christ and worshiped the Father in his name, and also we worship the Father in his name ... and for this cause it is sanctified unto us for righteousness, even as it was accounted unto Abraham in the wilderness to be obedient unto the commands of God in offering up his son Isaac, which is a similitude of God and his Only Begotten Son.[124]

Sacrifice is an eternal law which we are required to obey for individual exaltation. The prophet Joseph said, "The sacrifice required of Abraham in the offering up Isaac, shows that if a man would attain to the keys of the kingdom of an endless life; he must sacrifice all things."[125] The same was true for Sarah, who is the only woman in the Bible whose age, death, and burial are distinctly noted. She was the mother of the covenant race, a virtuous woman who was indeed a crown to her husband and a delight to the Lord. Abraham and Sarah accomplished every requirement necessary to reach the full measure of their creation, the fullness of the everlasting covenant, which is that "all that [the] Father hath shall be given unto [them],"[126] and every individual that becomes the seed of Abraham can achieve the same.[127]

Like father Adam, Abraham gave both mortal and spiritual blessings to his family shortly before his death. He blessed Isaac's sons, Jacob and Esau, Jacob's twelve sons,[128] and Ishmael's "twelve princes," all of whom would establish nations.[129] The last of Abraham's children came when he took Keturah to wife and they were blessed with six sons.[130]

Joseph Smith and Abraham

Abraham and Joseph Smith Jr. were two of the greatest mortal disciples of Jehovah/Jesus Christ who ever lived. They were both present in the great councils of the premortal world and both were foreordained as heads of dispensations. Their trial and test during mortality were very similar. (See Appendix B, "Abraham and Joseph.") Both of these exalted prophets will be major participants at Adam-ondi-Ahman when the Savior and father Adam meet with the elect of God. Both will rule and reign in the highest celestial realm of the kingdom of God. The same beautiful blessing pronounced upon Abraham regarding the inhabitants of the earth was also given to Joseph. "And as I said unto Abraham concerning the kindred of the earth, even so I say unto my servant Joseph: In thee and in thy seed shall the kindred of the earth be blessed."[131] As advocates for the doctrine of Christ in mortality, both men were appointed to receive revelation from the Lord for their dispensation. Of all the descendants of Adam and Eve, possibly none will give a better account of their stewardship of teaching Jehovah/Jesus Christ than these two prophets: Abraham to his posterity and circle of influence, and Joseph to the world.

Joseph Smith received great insight about Abraham through his translation of the Book of Mormon[132] and the Old and New Testaments. In the Bible so much becomes more evident in the JST version of Genesis 14, 15, 17, and 21. One significant change Joseph made vividly illustrates his understanding of Jehovah's relationship to Abraham and the patriarchal fathers. Exodus 6:3 reads: "And I appeared unto Abraham, unto Isaac, and unto Jacob, *by the name of God Almighty, but by my name JEHOVAH was I not known to them.*"

Joseph Smith's translation reads: "*I am the Lord God Almighty; the Lord Jehovah. And was not my name known unto them?*" (italics added). The world still believes the name Jehovah was not known until the time of Moses.

Through these translations, Joseph had a wealth of knowledge about Abraham before he received the papyri scrolls and facsimiles. This included an understanding of Abraham and Sarah from Doctrine and Covenants 132. With this knowledge, and with the aid of the Urim and Thummim, Joseph was able to recognize immediately that the papyri were the work of Abraham. Joseph's excitement must have been extremely high when he discovered the first verse of the translation identified the book as Abraham's. Is it possible that Joseph even recognized the hieroglyph signature of Abraham when he looked at the facsimiles? The hieroglyph symbol which identifies Abraham is found in each of the three facsimiles.

Abraham and Joseph had much in common when it came to communicating with heaven. Both eventually enjoyed

> the privilege of receiving the mysteries of the kingdom of heaven, to have the heavens opened unto them, to commune with the general assembly and church of the Firstborn, and to enjoy the communion and presence of God the Father, and Jesus the mediator of the new covenant.[133]

Abraham was among the forty or more messengers God sent to the prophet of this final dispensation.[134] President John Taylor testified that Abraham visited Joseph.

> I know of what I speak for I was very well acquainted with him (Joseph), and was with him a great deal during his life, and was with him when he died. The principles which he had, placed him in communication with the Lord, and not only with the Lord but with the ancient apostles and prophets; such men, for instance as Abraham.... He seemed to be as familiar with these people as we are with one another.[135]

One can only speculate as to what transpired on these visits. We know that Moroni visited Joseph over twenty times and instructed him at length on those occasions.[136] Joseph may have very well said to Abraham what Abraham said to Melchizedek: "I believe all that thou hast taught to me concerning the priesthood and the coming of the Son of Man."[137]

How wonderful it would be to have been privy to their conversations as they discussed their common knowledge and experiences, each expanding on such subjects as the grand council of the Gods[138] or the attempt of the adversary to destroy them at an early age, as he had tried to destroy Moses and the Savior. They could have discussed their first visions at fourteen years of age,[139] or their incarceration in the hellish jails of Missouri and Kardi and Kutha.[140]

Divine knowledge played a very important part in both men's lives. Father Abraham, already a man of great knowledge, personally pleaded with the Lord for greater knowledge.[141] Joseph Smith, after eighteen years of heavenly tutoring, was told while in Liberty Jail in March of 1839,

> God shall give unto you knowledge by his Holy Spirit, yea, by the unspeakable gift of the Holy Ghost, that has not been revealed since the world was until now; Which our forefathers have awaited with anxious expectation to be revealed in the last times, which their minds were pointed to by the angels, as held in reserve for the fulness of their glory.[142]

Abraham was the father of the covenant of divine redemption; Joseph was the revealer of the covenant to this final dispensation. Both received all ordinances of the everlasting covenant. Both held the keys for becoming "kings and priests of the Most High God" and received the fullness of the priesthood ordinances, even "the keys of the kingdom of an endless life."[143] In their stewardship, Abraham was the patriarch–father of the seed, while Joseph was the prophet to disperse the promised blessings to Abraham's descendants throughout the world. Abraham is a god.[144] Joseph holds the keys in heaven for the last dispensation. These crowning glories

came because both sacrificed sufficiently and fulfilled their foreordination as awesome revealors of Jehovah/Jesus Christ to their
dispensations. Both names are known throughout the world. Father
Abraham has been known through the centuries. Joseph's name is
rapidly spreading throughout the world in the latter days.

Summary

To Abraham, Sarah, and their posterity, blessings came as they
were faithful and true to their roles in mortality to which they
were foreordained in the premortal world. This eternal unit lived
up to every trust that the Gods of heaven placed in them. Their
life together consolidated a fullness of all ordinances from baptism
to the fullness. They enjoyed the full endowment of blessings and
sealings, receiving all keys and ordinances of the priesthood in the
proper sequence in their dispensation. Abraham ultimately received
the promise that these blessings would be available to all of his
posterity.[145] Hence, the keys of the dispensation of the gospel of
Abraham in its fullness, with the patriarchal order of the priesthood, was restored in our time and equates to the "dispensation of
the gospel of Abraham."

Understanding the works of Abraham and Sarah is a supernal quest
for those in mortality. To members of The Church of Jesus Christ
of Latter-day Saints, Abraham and Sarah are the great prototypes
of patriarch and matriarch, knowledge and righteousness. Their
steadfastness and undaunted spirits in overcoming trials of faith,
their sacrifices unto the Lord, their loyalty to family, and their
personal integrity are examples that should be imitated. Scriptural admonitions to "become the seed of Abraham," obtain to
"Abraham's bosom," and "go and do the works of Abraham" are
simply telling us to follow their example and work to attain the
measure of our creation, even the highest degree of celestial glory,
which is the fullness of the everlasting covenant. Hence, a study,
pondering and understanding of Book of Abraham with its three
facsimiles seems critical.

Chapter 2:
The Book of Abraham

*"A Translation of some Ancient Records that have fallen into
our hands, from the Catacombs of Egypt, purporting to be the writings
of Abraham, while he was in Egypt, called the Book of Abraham,
written by his own hand upon papyrus."*

—Commentary on the papyri by Joseph Smith.

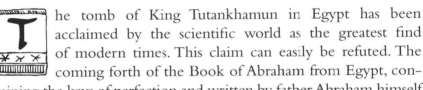 he tomb of King Tutankhamun in Egypt has been acclaimed by the scientific world as the greatest find of modern times. This claim can easily be refuted. The coming forth of the Book of Abraham from Egypt, containing the keys of perfection and written by father Abraham himself to his seed, would have to be considered the find of greatest worth. (See "Tutankhamun" and "1851 First Edition Book of Abraham.") The substantiation of this claim is best explained by referring to the last two verses of the Old Testament and the second section of the Doctrine and Covenants. At the close of one great book of scripture and in the opening verses of another, a great condemnation is declared on the inhabitants of the earth if they do not establish a proper relationship with the fathers. First, the Lord will "come and smite the earth with a curse,"[1] and second, "the whole earth would be utterly wasted at his coming."[2] In chapter one, verse two of his book, father Abraham explains how these condemnations can be avoided. "And, finding there was greater happiness and peace and rest for me, I sought for the blessings of the fathers, and the right whereunto I should be ordained to administer the same." In this verse, father Abraham describes how to receive the blessings

Tutankhamun

rather than the curses. The Book of Abraham and the facsimiles contained therein fully describe the blessings of the fathers and how they can be obtained, thereby preventing the whole earth from being wasted at the Lord's coming.

The Book of Abraham was written by father Abraham and has been canonized as the word of God. The great scholar and Egyptologist Hugh B. Nibley said: "So when we read 'The Book of Abraham, written by his own hand upon papyrus,' we are to understand, as the Mormons always have, that this book no matter how often 'renewed' is still the writing of Abraham and no one else; for he commissioned it or 'according to the accepted Egyptian expression' wrote it himself—with his own hand. And when Abraham tells us, 'That you may have an understanding of these gods, I have given you the fashion of them in the figures at the beginning,' we do not need to imagine the patriarch himself personally drawing the very sketches we have before us. In fact, the remark may well be the insertion of a later scribe. To the Egyptian or Hebrew mind the sketches could be twenty-seventh hand and still be the authentic originals, as long as Abraham originally ordered them and put his name to them."[3]

It was the responsibility of Abraham as God's representative to pass on to our dispensation the keys and authority of the patriarchal order of the Melchizedek Priesthood which enable a family to perfect themselves and their posterity. Abraham employed much of what he had learned in Ur and Egypt to accomplish this divine errand. He knew that the first Pharaoh had imitated the order that had been established by the fathers.[4] The quest of the Egyptians and their apostate methods of obtaining the afterworld were found in

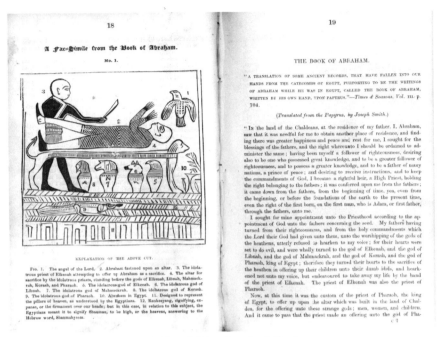

1851 First Edition Book of Abraham

their writings: the Pyramid Texts, Coffin Texts, and the Book of the Dead. These texts, which were thought to be magic spells, were in truth remnants of the order of God and have a real kinship to what is found in both the Old and New Testaments as to the Godhead, covenants, revelation, and life after death. Abraham presented much of the fullness of the order of God by using the facsimiles in conjunction with the written word in the Book of Abraham to convey to our dispensation the truth of the everlasting covenant. (See Chapter 3, "The Everlasting Covenant.") Prominent Egyptologists of our day view each of the facsimiles as "a structure of real significance, the true value of their message still awaiting discovery."[5]

Abraham's knowledge about Egyptian drawings would have come from experiences he had with the Egyptian hierarchy and their scribes, who wrote and read hieroglyphs. A great blessing to his ministry was that these hieroglyphs were found all through Ur and Egypt and with slight modification could be used effectively to

Egyptian coffins containing mummies

teach gospel principles. The Book of Abraham, with its symbolic facsimiles, depicts a verbal and visual representation of truth in a beautiful way.

Church history states: "On the 3rd of July [1835], Michael H. Chandler came to Kirtland [Ohio] to exhibit some Egyptian mummies. There were four human figures, together with some two or more rolls [scrolls] of papyrus covered with hieroglyphic figures and devices."[6] These were purchased for $2,400. Joseph Smith translated the Book of Abraham from one of these scrolls.[7] They had been taken out of tombs and catacombs in the Valley of the Kings located on the west bank of the Nile River at Thebes around 1818–1821. Several of the mummified bodies purchased were identified through examination and comparison with mummies in the London Museum which had been found at the same time.[8] (See picture of comparable Egyptian coffins.) We know from the quality of the embalming that these bodies were of Egyptian nobility. The body of Abraham was not among them, as he was buried in the cave of Machpelah in Canaan.

While the bulk of these scrolls were destroyed in the Chicago Fire of 1871, eleven fragments and one facsimile from the original scrolls survived. In the original scrolls the facsimiles were together but were later cut apart before being sold.[9] These fragments were obtained by The Church of Jesus Christ of Latter-day Saints from the Metropolitan Museum of Art in 1967, and from these, the scrolls were identified as Hor, Tsemmin, Noufianoub, and Amenhotep.[10]

It is rather interesting that there is not a consensus among LDS scholars on dates or even the period when Joseph actually translated the Book of Abraham. H. Donl Peterson gives one set of dates, but does not delineate between Joseph's work on the Egyptian alphabet and the translation of the book itself.[11] John Gee declared that Joseph started the translation immediately upon receiving the scrolls and finished the work in November of 1835. He illustrates this in a "Translation time line."[12] Hugh Nibley seems to have cleared up the matter by employing the times used by the Church Historian's Office. He concludes, "We nowhere find mention of Joseph Smith engaged in translating the Book of Abraham itself before October of 1840."[13] At various times Joseph shared information about Abraham, but earlier work on the scrolls related only to the "Egyptian alphabet." Real translation of the book was accomplished in 1841. It really makes no difference as far as doctrine is concerned. We have the book and know that Joseph translated it; however, Dr. Nibley's conclusion that the work was started in 1840 supports our previous premise that the Book of Abraham was part of the important knowledge the Lord was referring to when he told Joseph in 1839, "God shall give unto you knowledge . . . that has not been revealed since the world was until now."[14] Since Joseph translated the Book of Abraham after his incarceration in Liberty Jail, the contents of the book become part of this knowledge.[15]

One can almost imagine the joy and exhilaration Joseph felt upon obtaining the art and the scrolls. Not only did he get another glimpse into the world of the patriarchs, but he also received gospel truths from father Abraham himself. On 16 December 1835, Joseph wrote, "I exhibited and explained the Egyptian records to them [William E. M'Lellin, Brigham Young, and Jared Carter], and explained many things concerning the dealing of God with the ancients, and the formation of the planetary system." With W. W. Phelps and Oliver Cowdery as scribes, Joseph "commenced the translation of some of the characters or hieroglyphics, and much

to our joy found that one of the rolls contained the writings of
Abraham [by his own hand while he was in Egypt]" and also the
writings of Joseph of Egypt.[16] Concerning the records of Abraham,
Joseph Smith said:

> The record ... is beautifully written on papyrus, with black,
> and a small part red, ink or paint, in perfect preservation. The
> characters are such as you find upon the coffins of mummies—
> hieroglyphics, etc.; with many characters of letters like the
> present ... form of the Hebrew without points.

One month later Joseph showed this record to Rabbi Joshua Seixas,
who "pronounced it original."[17] Nephi, in the beginning of the
Book of Mormon, described the language he would use to write
his history: "Yea, I make a record in the language of my father,
which consists of the learning of the Jews and the language of the
Egyptians."[18]

These Abrahamic records caused great excitement among the Saints
from the beginning. W. W. Phelps in a letter to his wife, Sally
Waterman Phelps, dated July 19 and 20, 1835, wrote:

> The last of June four Egyptian mummies were brought here;
> there were two papyrus rolls, besides some other ancient
> Egyptian writings with them ... they were presented to President
> Smith. He soon knew what they were and said they, the 'rolls
> of papyrus,' contained the sacred record kept of Joseph in
> Pharaoh's court in Egypt, and the teachings of Father Abraham.
> God has so ordained it that these mummies and writings have
> been brought in the Church, and the sacred writing I had just
> locked up in Brother Joseph's house when your letter came.
> There is nothing secret or hidden that shall not be revealed, and
> they come to the Saints.[19]

The writings of Joseph, Abraham's great-grandson who spent his
entire adult life in Egypt, were not translated. It is probable from
what Joseph Smith said about Joseph keeping the record in Egypt,
and from what Brother Nibley has said, that Joseph of Egypt had
some input on his great-grandfather's work.[20]

Why are the writings of Abraham so important? Since the beginning of time, Elohim, Jehovah, and the Holy Ghost have entered into covenants with mortal man. (See Chapter 3, "The Everlasting Covenant.") Abraham's dispensation received a complete understanding of gospel covenants.[21] The Book of Abraham is part of the evidence of what the Lord told Abraham—that he would "make of thee a great nation and I will bless thee, and make thy name great; and thou shalt be a blessing."[22] In the Book of Mormon, Nephi gives us further insight:

> Wherefore, our father hath not spoken of our seed alone, but also of all the house of Israel, pointing to the covenant which should be fulfilled in the latter days; which covenant the Lord made to our father Abraham, saying: In thy seed shall all the kindred of the earth be blessed.[23]

A need for the writings and works of father Abraham is emphasized in the New Testament when Jesus, speaking to Abraham's seed, said, "And ye do that which ye have seen with your father. They answered and said unto him, Abraham is our father. Jesus saith unto them, If ye were Abraham's children, ye would do the works of Abraham."[24] Certainly the Book of Abraham helps members of the Church to understand the works of Abraham.

A second witness to the importance of knowing and understanding the works of Abraham is contained in the Doctrine and Covenants. On 12 July 1843, Joseph finally recorded a revelation relating to the new and everlasting covenant which included the eternal nature of the marriage covenant and specified why the writings of Abraham were so necessary: "Go ye, therefore, and do the works of Abraham; enter ye into my law and ye shall be saved."[25] Without the Book of Abraham, our understanding of this law would be limited, as would our understanding of the full tapestry of the everlasting covenant.

These beautiful writings of Abraham are also part of the fulfillment of the prophecy the Lord gave to Nephi: "I will be merciful unto the Gentiles in that day, insomuch that I will bring forth unto them, in mine own power, much of my gospel, which shall be plain and precious, saith the Lamb."[26] The Book of Abraham, with its facsimiles, really is plain and precious.

One of the highlights of the Book of Abraham is that it provides strong scriptural evidence of pre-earth life in its description of premortal activities among the spirits of mankind. It presents knowledge about the house of Israel, the Lord's chosen people, and an understanding of the planetary system and the creation of the earth. It speaks of the nature of man, individual valiancy, and gradation in all things. In chapter three, Abraham talks about time. He uses the terms "set time" and the "same order as that upon which thou standest." Dr. Nibley, speaking of time, said, "This is one of the mysteries of cosmology today."[27] The facsimiles illustrate through Egyptian writing specific powers of the Godhead, how this authority is conveyed to earth, even the "keys of the dispensation of the gospel of Abraham." There is also information on personal perfection, the coronation of the sons and daughters of God, and the eternal nature of the family.

President John Taylor said of the Book of Abraham: "It is a power of eternal truth and its doctrine is the greatest boon that could be conferred upon man; the offspring of heaven, the gift of the Gods, a celestial treasure, an earthly, heavenly inheritance, a living, abiding, and eternal reality."[28] Joseph identifies the writings as a welcome confirmation of his own ideas, but never as the source of those ideas. Even when "the principles of astronomy as understood by father Abraham and the ancients, unfolded to our understandings, it was by direct revelation and not by our understandings,…it was by direct revelation and not by reading the text."[29] The Book of Abraham, with its facsimiles, helps one better understand the mysteries of godliness. Joseph revealed the key to the mysteries of godliness when he said:

> Here then is eternal life—to know the only wise and true God. You have got to learn how to make yourselves Gods in order to save yourselves and be kings and priests to God. The same

as all Gods have done—by going from a small capacity to a great capacity, from a small degree to another, from grace to grace, ... from exaltation to exaltation—till you are able to sit in everlasting burnings and everlasting power and glory as those who have gone before, sit enthroned.[30]

The Book of Abraham was first published in the 1 March 1842 *Times and Seasons*. On this same day, Joseph Smith made an entry in his journal which read: "During the forenoon I was at my office, correcting the first plate or cut of the records of Father Abraham ... and in the evening with the Twelve and their wives at Elder Woodruff's, at which time I explained many important principles in relation to progressive improvement in the scale of intelligent existence."[31]

It is interesting that section 132 of the Doctrine and Covenants, which tells about the dispensation of father Abraham, Isaac, and Jacob and their wives, called at this time "the eternal marriage doctrine," was published with the Book of Abraham in the 1878 edition to make this doctrine more accessible to the Saints. This section sets forth instructions for eternal progression[32] and conditions of the new and everlasting covenant[33] necessary to obtain godhood.[34] These truths are so necessary in a world where "all their creeds were an abomination in" the sight of the Lord.[35]

The Prophet Joseph Smith summarized the Book of Abraham and, particularly, the facsimiles this way:

The organization of the spiritual and heavenly worlds, and of spiritual and heavenly beings, was agreeable to the most perfect order and harmony; their limits and bounds were fixed irrevocably, and voluntarily subscribed to in their heavenly estate by themselves, and were by our first parents subscribed to upon the earth. Hence the importance of embracing and subscribing to principles of eternal truth by all men [men is used figuratively to include both sexes] upon the earth that expect eternal life.[36]

The Book of Abraham and the facsimiles are vital parts of the doctrine of Christ. An understanding of the works of Abraham is critical for the progression of the seed of Abraham—members of The Church of Jesus Christ of Latter-day Saints. As "the seed of Abraham" through ordinances,[37] they must believe what Abraham believed, worship as Abraham worshiped, and be one with him in spiritual attributes, for "if ye be Christ's then are ye Abraham's seed, and heirs according to the promise."[38]

Chapter 3:
The Everlasting Covenant

resident Joseph F. Smith declared that Father in heaven has bestowed "upon us the richest of all blessings that man can enjoy in this life—the Holy Spirit and a knowledge of the new and everlasting covenant."[1] Elder Erastus Snow gave this beautiful and profound explanation of the covenant:

> This new and everlasting covenant reveals unto us the keys of the Holy Priesthood and ordinances thereof. It is the grand keystone of the arch which the Lord is building in the earth. In other words, it is that which completes the exaltation and glory of the righteous who receive the everlasting Gospel, and without it they could not attain unto the eternal power and Godhead and the fullness of celestial glory. They cannot progress through the ceaseless rounds of eternity except they abide in the covenant, and abide the law that governs it.[2]

Covenants, then, provide a means whereby God can give man ordinances, commandments, and eternal laws to bring about man's redemption through his agency to accept or reject.

After completing the translation of the Book of Abraham and prior to printing the facsimiles, Joseph Smith said it was Abraham's record that informed him about the everlasting covenant made between three personages before this earth was created.[3] These three personages are titled God the Creator, God the Redeemer, and God the Testator. The everlasting covenant was given to Adam and Eve, and it was taught to their family down to and even through Abraham, Isaac, and Jacob. Being new to our dispensation, it is now called the new and everlasting covenant. Father in heaven, "God the Creator," whom we worship, implemented the covenant. The covenant receives efficacy from the atonement of Jesus Christ, "God the Redeemer," whose sacrifice embraces, sustains, supports, and gives life and force to the doctrine of the gospel, for it is the foundation upon which all truth rests and all things grow out of.[4] The testifying of knowledge, powers, blessings, and sealings of the covenant is brought about by the Holy Ghost, "God the Testator."

It is in the everlasting covenant that the three members of the Godhead are one as proclaimed in scripture and depicted through symbol and explanation in Facsimile 2. Symbols of the three members of the Godhead, distinct and separate, are found in almost every Christian culture and society. (See "The Castillo," "Sacred altar with three panels" and "Native American sacred Ojibwa birch bark writings" on opposite page.) Members of The Church of Jesus Christ of Latter-day Saints know that one has to be in covenant with the Father to enjoy the blessing of eternal life. They know they have to be in covenant with the Son to become part of His church and kingdom. And they certainly know they must be in covenant with the Holy Ghost to enjoy His companionship continually and be privileged to His gifts. President Joseph F. Smith put it this way: "Not only is it necessary to have faith in God, but also in Jesus Christ, his Son, the Savior of mankind and the Mediator of the New Covenant: and in the Holy Ghost, who bears record of the Father and the Son, 'the same in all ages and forever.' "[5]

The everlasting covenant was first explained in the grand council of heaven prior to the Creation. During pre-earth life the eternal laws of the plan of salvation were carefully explained. Those spirit children who supported the plan made their first everlasting covenants while in the spirit world. Those who were obedient and

The Castillo, Tulum, Mexico
Three panels—God of Heaven, Descending God, Blank God—above three doors

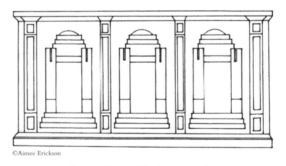

©Aimee Erickson

Sacred altar with three panels

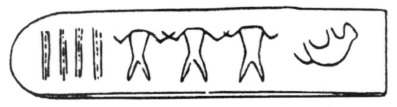

Native American sacred Ojibwa birch bark writings, panel of three

faithful in keeping them received the status of elect and started the
process of making their election sure in mortality.[6] Those who want
to return to God and be with Him, and have their own individual
mortal families preserved as a part of that eternal patriarchal order
of the Gods, must receive and be faithful to all the ordinances
within the everlasting covenant while in mortality.[7]

The conditions of this everlasting covenant, or "Law of God,"[8] are
that

> all covenants, contracts, bonds, obligations, oaths, vows,
> performances, connections, associations, or expectations, that
> are not made and entered into and sealed by the Holy Spirit
> of promise ... for time and for all eternity, ... are of no efficacy,
> virtue, or force in and after the resurrection from the dead; for
> all contracts that are not made unto this end have an end when
> men are dead.[9]

Covenants are the channels for the divine power of the Melchizedek
Priesthood within the eternal kingdom of God on earth and in
heaven. All that comprises the everlasting covenant is the mortar of
the foundation of the plan of salvation, the plan of happiness, even
the plan of redemption.[10]

The holy scriptures encompass and expound the everlasting
covenant. The word *covenant* appears in the Old Testament at least
273 times and is the heart and continuous theme of the Hebrew
Bible. It appears in the New Testament thirty-two times, wherein
the old and new covenants are explained and compared.[11] The
word *testament* means "covenant." In the Russian Bible the Old
Testament is called the Old Covenant and New Testament is called
the New Covenant. *Covenant* appears in the Book of Mormon 155
times. One of the purposes of the Book of Mormon, as declared
on the title page, is "that they may know the covenants of the
Lord." *Covenant* appears in the Doctrine and Covenants ninety-
four times—first in the title, and then in the introduction, in which
the Lord declares: "That mine everlasting covenant might be established; that the fulness of my gospel might be proclaimed." It also

states that the anger of the Lord is kindled because "they have strayed from mine ordinances, and have broken mine everlasting covenant."[12] It closes with, "And this shall be our covenant, that we will walk in all the ordinances of the Lord."[13] In the Pearl of Great Price, *covenant* is found seven times, each time in relationship to a major gospel dispensation. Finally, much knowledge about the covenant is depicted within the three facsimiles of the Book of Abraham.

The everlasting covenant was introduced to Adam and Eve in mortality when they embraced the first principles of the gospel, which are faith, repentance, baptism, and the gift of the Holy Ghost.[14] The Book of Mormon tells us that the Atonement and covenant blessings apply only to those who are the descendants of Adam and Eve,[15] and for their posterity, these benefits will extend past mortality into the eternities. (See Appendix F, "An Eternity.")

This everlasting covenant of the Godhead has been taught in every dispensation,[16] as indicated in the facsimiles, but has not been available in its fullness to every individual. Speaking of our day and our dispensation, the prophet Ezekiel said that God would establish "an everlasting covenant with them and I will...set my sanctuary in the midst of them for evermore."[17] Our dispensation of the fullness of times has been blessed with a complete restoration. All ordinances are available to every righteous and worthy Saint on both sides of the veil; hence, the necessity of genealogy and vicarious temple work. Entering into the everlasting covenant places an individual in covenant with Father, Son, and Holy Ghost,[18] and they become a son or daughter of Christ. The individual becomes spiritually alive, acquiring the potential power to return as a son or daughter of Father upon fulfillment of all of the ordinances.

The ordinance sequence is baptism, confirmation, priesthood, endowment, celestial marriage, and ordinances of the fullness of the priesthood. Step by step, it is a rebirth process of being cleansed through the blood of Christ and sanctified by the Holy Spirit. Inherent to the marriage ordinance was the necessity of restoring the patriarchal order of the Melchizedek Priesthood. The dispensation of the gospel of Abraham, containing the keys of the patriarchal order of the Melchizedek Priesthood, were restored in the Kirtland Temple. The power of these keys established the authority for perfecting the Saints, or "to perfect the saints through the ordinances of the House of the Lord."[19] In fact, *perfection* means to complete or abide the covenant.[20] God's covenant of exaltation (eternal marriage) is the gate that leads to the highest glory of the celestial kingdom. The gospel is the everlasting covenant because it is ordained by Him who is everlasting and also because it is everlastingly the same. It is new to everyone who accepts it. Hence, the gospel and its ordinances are the new and everlasting covenant.

There are usually only two ordinances performed in the name of the Father and of the Son and of the Holy Ghost which are heard by an individual while in mortality. The first is the ordinance of baptism, which puts the individual in covenant with all three members of the Godhead. It is the key to the celestial kingdom. This ordinance of salvation is new and everlasting to the individual. The covenant is singular and individual, and without further ordinances one would end in the first heaven or glory of the celestial kingdom.

The second ordinance performed in the name of all three members of the Godhead is the ordinance of exaltation. It is the celestial marriage of two individuals who seek the highest heaven within the celestial kingdom. This ordinance is only performed for a worthy son and daughter who have the joint desire to become one with each other and with the Father, the Son, and the Holy Ghost through eternal covenants, with the potential of receiving and enjoying with the members of the Godhead all that they have.[21] Every aspect of the everlasting covenant is of transcendent significance, for it marshals and energizes within those in covenant enormous powers—the ability to live, complete, and finish every promise made within the everlasting covenant.

Abraham's facsimiles could be called the picture tutorials of the everlasting covenant, while Doctrine and Covenants 132 would be the written revelation that explains it. Verses 2-4 of section 132 speak of entering into the glory of the Gods through the everlasting covenant. Verse 5 verifies what Joseph learned in the record of Abraham, that the covenant originated before the foundation of the world. Verse 6 tells the world that "it was instituted for the fulness of my [God's] glory." The covenant is defined in verse 7, and we are told of the three instigators of the covenant in verses 11 and 18. Verses 19 and 29 tell of the coronation that Facsimile 3 illustrates. We find that eternal lives can be gained by understanding the Gods and receiving the law in verse 24. Verse 32 declares which work is the greatest challenge for each mortal. Verse 36 explains the righteousness Abraham so earnestly sought.[22] Verse 49 defines the fulness of the priesthood, while verse 50 illustrates the necessity of sacrifice. Verse 63 explains part of Jehovah's covenant to the Father, and verses 65 and 66 define the "Law of Sarah." To understand the three facsimiles of the Book of Abraham, one should be familiar with and understand this section in the Doctrine and Covenants. Joseph Smith said he could quote this revelation (section 132) of the Doctrine and Covenants verbatim anytime he was asked to do so.[23] Hence, understanding the mysteries of God is necessary to becoming a god.[24] The scriptures declare, "The everlasting covenant was instituted for the fulness of my glory; and he that receiveth a fulness thereof must and shall abide the law ... saith the Lord God."[25] Understanding this section and this scripture gives an eternal scope to God's declaration, "This is my work and my glory—to bring to pass the immortality and eternal life of man."[26]

All the prophets have looked forward to the establishment of the everlasting covenant in our dispensation of the fullness of times.[27] Speaking of our days, Isaiah wrote, "Incline your ear, and come unto me: hear, and your soul shall live; and I will make an everlasting covenant with you."[28] For Abraham's seed, by birth or adoption, to be blessed, they must receive the ordinances and enter into the covenant and then with faithfulness endure to the end. The ordinances of the everlasting covenant will produce the measure of one's creation, even the fullness of the priesthood. Faith can produce it all. The apostle Paul states,

Know ye therefore that they which are of faith, the same are the children of Abraham. And the scripture, foreseeing that God would justify the heathen through faith, preached before the gospel unto Abraham, saying, In thee shall all the nations be blessed. So then they which be of faith are blessed with faithful Abraham.[29]

The Lord has said,

Verily I say unto you, blessed are you for receiving mine everlasting covenant, even the fulness of my gospel, sent forth unto the children of men, that they might have life and be made partakers of the glories which are to be revealed in the last days, as it was written by the prophets and apostles in days of old.[30]

George Q. Cannon, a counselor in the First Presidency, said,

Every member of the Church, young and old, should be taught to appreciate that to be admitted to covenant with God, to have communion of the Holy Ghost and to have the fellowship of the Saints, is the greatest honor and blessing that can be bestowed upon mortal man.[31]

At the present time, temples dot the earth, enabling the fullness of the everlasting covenant to be taken to almost every nation, kindred, tongue, and people. It is rapidly becoming possible for every faithful son and daughter of Christ "to hear the fulness of the gospel" in their own language.[32] This will continue until Isaiah's prophecy is fulfilled: "They shall not hurt nor destroy in all my holy mountain: for the earth shall be full of the knowledge of the LORD, as the waters cover the sea."[33] With this knowledge available to mortals, the warning of the Doctrine and Covenants becomes so profound:

Therefore, be not afraid of your enemies, for I have decreed in my heart, saith the Lord, that I will prove you in all things, whether you will abide in my covenant, even unto death, that you may be found worthy. For if ye will not abide in my covenant ye are not worthy of me.[34]

May we of the Church today declare as did the Saints at Winter Quarters, "And this shall be our covenant that we will walk in all the ordinances of the Lord."[35] President Boyd K. Packer said, "Ordinances and covenants become our credentials for admission into his presence. To worthily receive them is the quest of a lifetime; to keep them thereafter is the challenge of mortality." "Surely the Lord is pleased when we are worthy of the title: A keeper of the covenants."[36]

Chapter 4:
Three Facsimiles

T he three papyrus facsimiles were included with Abraham's scrolls and in the original followed each other sequentially.[1] Abraham knew that the concepts of Egyptian art encompassed truth, but the authority of priesthood powers were an imitation which had been present since the government of the first Pharaoh; he also knew that it was his errand from the Lord to teach correct principles with true authority. To do this, Abraham used modified illustrations within existing Egyptian facsimiles seen everywhere to teach correct principles to those who accepted and embraced the gospel. Abraham also made sure that the three facsimiles within his scrolls had the Egyptian art and writing necessary to convey to future saints the principles of divine truth that had been present since the time of father Adam. So we are blessed as a people and indebted to the Egyptians for their dedication to their deities and preserving that which they believed in a magnificent art form.

We may then ask, would it be any harder for Abraham to modify Egyptian art and make it pure than it would be for him, as a seer, to write the word of the Lord on an Egyptian scroll? Or would it be any harder for Joseph Smith to translate a facsimile rather than an Egyptian scroll? Abraham spent at least seven years, and possibly more, in Egypt, where he added to his knowledge of Egyptian art and the two forms of written language, hieratic and hieroglyphics. It is interesting that father Lehi and his posterity used a form of Egyptian in their records: "And now, behold, we have written this record according to our knowledge, in the characters which are called among us the reformed Egyptian, being handed down and altered by us, according to our manner of speech."[2] Abraham with authority of the true priesthood and illustrating art conveying correct principles, became so well known and respected in Egypt that "by the politeness of the king, with a crown on his head," he could sit on a throne emblematic of a true representative of God as illustrated in Facsimile No. 3.[3]

But to approach the facsimiles purely from the Egyptian-hieroglyphics background immediately moves one away from the doctrine of Christ. Rather than, "It must never be forgotten that we are dealing with a civilization thousands of years old and one of which only tiny remnants have survived," the approach should be, "We are dealing with a prophet's work about sacred, eternal doctrine that has been present from the beginning, and volumes of prophetic utterances along with scriptures explain these eternal truths." One's approach to the facsimiles should be the same as one's approach to the Book of Abraham. The figures and writings within each of the three facsimiles and their explanations disclose sacred, eternal doctrine in its simplest form and could be summarized as follows:

> **Facsimile 1**—represents priesthood principles and powers and illustrates the transmittal of these powers from heaven to earth.

> **Facsimile 2**—represents the heavenly and mortal participants of the everlasting covenant within a circle, all power in heaven and earth.

> **Facsimile 3**—represents a ritual coronation of covenanted sons and daughters of God.

The theme of the three facsimiles may be seen as corresponding to the Egyptians' version of their past, the present, and their future. They link pre-mortality to mortality to represent the past segment of eternal existence. They link mortal life with the powers of heaven, which represents the present. And finally, they illustrate the future, the glories of the eternities ahead. Referring to the facsimiles, Dr. Hugh Nibley said, "Egyptian hieroglyphic is not a naive picture-writing, but a special code governed by strict rules, without a knowledge of which it cannot be read."[4] We know that Father Abraham conveyed knowledge of eternal principles through these Egyptian motifs. In his writings he said, "and that you may have a knowledge of this altar, I will refer you to the representation at the commencement of this record." Remembering that in the original scrolls the three facsimiles were sequential, Abraham said, "That you may have an understanding of these gods, I have given you the fashion of them in the figures at the beginning, which manner of figures is called by the Chaldeans Rahleenos, which signifies hieroglyphics."[5]

From what Dr. Nibley has said, the Egyptians were obsessed with the subject of gods. "The mixing of gods and nations, especially those of Egypt and Canaan, was the order of the day in Abraham's time, and nowhere is the phenomenon more clearly in evidence than in the Book of Abraham."[6] When Abraham and Sarah arrived in Egypt they acquired a greater awareness of the hundreds of Egyptian gods. Abraham, of course, knew of the many idol gods of Israel, there being over five thousand idolatrous gods of Sumer alone. There were gods of Upper Egypt and Lower Egypt, gods of the four cardinal points, north, south, east, and west. In addition, each governmental area had its gods. It is interesting that most Egyptian gods were identified with a consort: Ra and Unas, Amen and Amen-Ra, Shu and Tefnut, Nau and Nen, Seb and Nut, Tem and Temp, and Het and Hepu. Many of the consorts are drawn in the form of the Egyptian goddess Hathor, believed to be the mother of life. Even though each worshiper claimed that his god was the father of all gods, it was Ra that was usually credited with being the father of all gods.

Of all the gods, Ra was considered the primeval and greatest god of the Egyptians. One inscription found frequently is "Since time of Ra," indicating that Ra had existed forever.[7] Ra was believed to be the possessor of seven souls and fourteen doubles. He was usually portrayed with the body of a man and the head of a hawk, probably an amalgamation from Henu, thought by some to be the first idol god of Egypt.[8] It was variations of these motifs and symbols, incorporated in each of the facsimiles, that Abraham used, and Joseph explained, to represent God the Creator, God the Redeemer, and God the Testator.

The most common secular conclusion about Abraham's facsimiles is exemplified by Samuel Birch. He said, "The esoteric meaning of these scenes is unknown."[9] On the other hand, Oliver Cowdery declared,

> The evidence is apparent…that they were written by persons acquainted with the history of the creation, the fall of man, and more or less of the correct ideas of notions of the Deity. The representation of the god-head—three, yet in one, is curiously drawn to give simply, though impressively, the writers views.[10]

Joseph had not translated the Book of Abraham at the time of this quote. Therefore, the source of Oliver's statement must have been from viewing and discussing the facsimiles. With this in mind, for members of the Church, the Lord's declaration seems timely: "And if it so be that the church is built upon my gospel then will the Father show forth his own works in it."[11]

The common threads to all three facsimiles are gods, angel, prophets, priests and kings, up-raised hands of supplication, offering-sacrifice altar, and the bound lotus plant. Other consistencies are the Utchat (Wedjat) Eye, a symbol of completeness and perfection; Hathor, universal mother; and truth—past, present, and future.[12] Also common are two genders with specific responsibilities—priesthood and creative powers—and four individual drawings representing both false gods and angels with keys and authority.

Although there are numerous parallels to Egyptian facsimiles that have inscriptions and glyphs showing similar scenes, Abraham's facsimiles are distinctively different. His coordinate and remain doctrinally harmonious with each other throughout the three facsimiles with a distinct message that is sequentially conveyed. One example is knowledge and authority that is transmitted from God to man, which is an eternal principle and conveyed in each facsimile. The truthfulness of each facsimile is the presence of the art form "Abraham in Egypt" in each one which certainly validates the work.

The knowledge contained in the facsimiles' motifs is symbolic in form. Symbols have multiple meanings for each individual. Each individual takes the fill of their understanding, but there is always more. This is illustrated in the Savior's feeding of the multitude. Each individual ate of the bread until they were filled, and yet there were many loaves left over. The knowledge of symbols, like partaking of the Lord's bread, is limitless. One must always look beyond the symbol for more understanding. First impressions generally come through the senses in multiple layers, followed by limitless knowledge from the Holy Spirit as decreed in the Doctrine and Covenants: "God shall give unto you knowledge by his Holy Spirit, yea, by the unspeakable gift of the Holy Ghost ... What power shall stay the heavens...to hinder the Almighty from pouring down knowledge from heaven upon the heads of the Latter-day Saints."[13] Abraham spoke by the Spirit, through symbols, and Joseph understood through divine inspiration.

There are symbols found in each of the facsimiles that are mysterious but sacred and, as Joseph said, can be found in the temple.[14] In fact, the Egyptian word for burial means "to initiate one in the mysteries." As his ultimate objective, the dead requests "permission to enter into the Holy of Holies of the Temple of Heliopolis" on the grounds that as an "Elder" he has been "initiated into the deepest secrets of the Temple."[15] This may very well be the reason father Abraham used both symbol and verse, and the combination had to come to the prophet Joseph. The knowledge of the facsimiles was paramount in enabling Joseph Smith to understand the importance of the temple. The Lord said concerning the Nauvoo Temple,

> Verily I say unto you, let this house be built unto my name, that I may reveal mine ordinances therein unto my people; For I deign to reveal unto my church things which have been kept hid from before the foundation of the world, things that pertain to the dispensation of the fulness of times. And I will *show* unto my servant Joseph all things pertaining to this house, and the priesthood thereof.[16]

The word *show* seems paramount.

These three facsimiles are part of the fulfillment of Abraham's ministry, as evidenced by another prophet who had a similar calling. Nephi said some twelve hundred years later,

> For the fulness of mine intent is that I may persuade men to come unto the God of Abraham, and the God of Isaac, and the God of Jacob, and be saved. Wherefore, the things which are pleasing unto the world I do not write, but the things which are pleasing unto God and unto those who are not of the world.[17]

The god of Abraham, Isaac, and Jacob is He who brought the fulness of the everlasting covenant to each one of them, producing what is called the covenant dispensation. These papyri truly verify that Abraham and Joseph were prophet revealers of the true and living God.

Chapter 5:
Facsimile No. 1

braham describes Facsimile No. 1 as a sacrificial scene with himself as the sacrifice, saying, "Therefore they turned their hearts to the sacrifice of the heathen in offering up their children unto these dumb idols, and hearkened not unto my voice, but endeavored to take away my life by the hand of the priest of Elkenah."[1] Two of the central principles of the plan of salvation (and two principles which are well illustrated in this facsimile) are the laws of obedience and sacrifice, which are prime components among the laws of God. Explaining the necessity of Abraham's required obedience sacrifice of Isaac, President George Q. Cannon explained why the Lord required this: "because He [Jehovah] intended to give him [Abraham] glory, exaltation and honor; He intended to make him a king and a priest, to share with Himself the glory, power and dominion which He exercised."[2] President Lorenzo Snow, speaking of the need for mortals to understand these principles, said,

> The Lord seems to require some proof on our part, something to show that He can depend upon us when He wants us to accomplish certain things in his interest. The reason is that the condition in which we will be placed in the future, as time passes along, as eternity approaches, and as we move forward in

Facsimile No. 1

Explanation (as given in the *Pearl of Great Price*):

Fig. 1   The Angel of the Lord

Fig. 2   Abraham fastened upon an altar

Fig. 3   The idolatrous priest of Elkenah attempting to offer up Abraham as a sacrifice

Fig. 4   The altar for sacrifice by the idolatrous priests, standing before the gods of
Elkenah, Libnah, Mahmackrah, Korash, and Pharaoh

Fig. 5   The idolatrous god of Elkenah

Fig. 6   The idolatrous god of Libnah

Fig. 7   The idolatrous god of Mahmackrah

Fig. 8   The idolatrous god of Korash

Fig. 9   The idolatrous god of Pharaoh

Fig. 10 Abraham in Egypt

Fig. 11 Designed to represent the pillars of heaven, as understood by the Egyptians

Fig. 12 Raukeeyang, signifying expanse, or the firmament over our heads; but in
this case, in relation to this subject, the Egyptians meant it to signify Shaumau,
to be high, or the heavens, answering to the Hebrew word, Shaumahyeem

eternity and along the line of our existence, we shall be placed in certain conditions that require very great sacrifice in the interests of humanity, in the interests of the Spirit of God, in the interest of His children and our own children, in generations to come, in eternity.[3]

Does sacrifice mean giving up one's life? No, not in the sense of death, but in giving up one's life to the Lord, to His work, to the family, to mankind, to make all the sacrifices necessary to obtain all that Abraham has received. The Lord has indicated to us in the Book of Mormon a type and shadow of the sacrifice that will save us from this idolatrous world: "I would that ye should come unto Christ, …Yea, come unto him, and offer your whole souls as an offering unto him, … and endure to the end; and as the Lord liveth ye will be saved."[4]

Another central theme of this facsimile is "spiritual communication." It is through the ordinances of the everlasting covenant "that the rights of the priesthood are inseparably connected with the powers of heaven, and … the powers of heaven cannot be controlled nor handled only upon the principles of righteousness."[5] The facsimile illustrates that the doors of heaven are always open to the righteous sons and daughters of God, and prayers are answered for those who ask, seek, and knock. Abraham's own narration of the events depicted in this facsimile clearly illustrate this principle. He said,

> And as they lifted up their hands upon me, that they might offer me up and take away my life, behold, I lifted up my voice unto the Lord my God, and the Lord hearkened and heard, and he filled me with the vision of the Almighty, and the angel of his presence stood by me, and immediately unloosed my bands; And his voice was unto me: Abraham, Abraham, behold, my name is Jehovah, and I have heard thee, and have come down to deliver thee, and to take thee away from thy father's house, and from all thy kinsfolk, into a strange land which thou knowest not of.[6]

This facsimile illustrates that the powers and knowledge of heaven are available to covenant mortals on earth, which literally constitutes an endowment of power from on high as spiritual knowledge from heaven is transferred to mortal biological offspring.

In this facsimile, opposition in all things, including the conflict between good and evil, is also clearly illustrated. Satan is the father of opposition to the plan of salvation, a truth continuously echoed through the scriptures. Since the beginning, the adversary through "darkness and temptation" has attempted to thwart the plan of salvation.[7] The devil and his forces are the source of all unrighteousness. Satan, by his very nature, uses cunning, deceit, and lies to influence and persuade men to do evil. He corrupts societies and laws, and through evil disciples tries to persuade all men to do evil. The Book of the Revelation of Abraham, an old Slavic pseudepigrapha manuscript found in the University of Moscow in Russia, gives a vivid dialogue on the reality of the forces of evil, speaking specifically of Abraham. "And when I (Abraham) heard the bird speak, I said to the angel: 'What is this my Lord?' and he answered: 'This is godlessness, this is Azazel [the idolatrous priest].'" The messenger angel Iaoel then said to the angel Azazel,

> the Strong One the Primeval One, the Ruler made thee an earth-dweller, and through thee every evil spirit of lies; and made also through thee anger, and vexation among the races of godless men; but God ... Almighty, has not permitted that the bodies of the righteous should be in thy power, thereby the life of the righteous is secured as well as the destruction of the wicked...Thy enmity is righteousness. Therefore, because of thy perdition, vanish before me![8]

The text goes on to say the evil angel Azazel left because Abraham had followed all that had been taught him by Iaoel. Abraham would also have been knowledgeable about Apep, the Egyptian god-enemy of Ra, the crocodile of the underworld shown as Figure 9 at the bottom of this facsimile. This evil god, like Ra, had many names. Apep was usually pictured as a serpent, but sometimes as a croco-

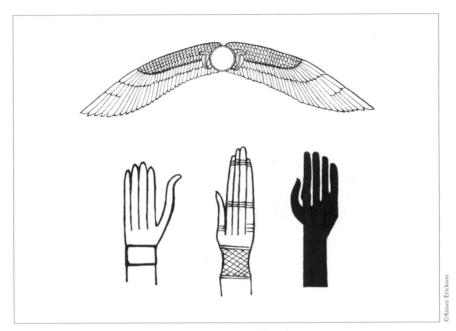

Egyptian wings and hands

dile. It was believed that the evil one, Apep, could be destroyed by reciting specific words of power.[9]

In this facsimile the forces of evil—priest, lion, knife, crocodile and the four false gods—all show the man on the couch to be in grave jeopardy. (The four false gods of evil here are used to represent another concept, as shown in Figure 6 of Facsimile No. 2.) All other figures are forces of good, being invested with divine power to save life. These figures face in the opposite direction, a vivid contrast of good and evil representing opposition in all things.[10] Those facing right represent true concepts of the "Plan of Redemption"—the prophet Abraham, heavenly messengers, and angels with sealing powers. Those who destroy life and represent evil—the false priest, the lion table, the crocodile—are facing left. This facsimile also illustrates plainly that the forces of righteousness crushed evil, and victory was theirs. The Lord protects His own, but the devil allows his own to be destroyed. It also is a reminder that God tries us; Satan seduces us. This is a continuation of the scenario between the

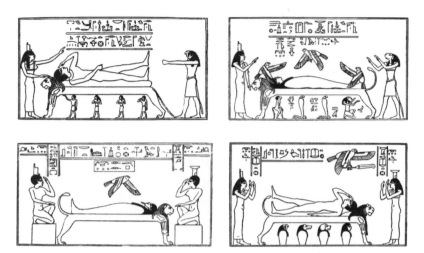

Lion couch scenes

Father and Lucifer which began in the pre-mortal world. The ever-lasting covenant provides every endowed soul of Abraham's posterity with an important understanding of Satan's enmity towards the works and people of God and the power that members of the Church possesses over him through the powers of the atonement and resurrection of Jesus Christ.

The changes to this facsimile from Egyptian norm can be seen clearly through careful comparisons. These modifications from more typical Egyptian art include the lotus-plant altar that Joseph said represents Abraham. This motif of Abraham is slightly different in all three facsimiles, but does identify Abraham, as Joseph has declared in his explanation. This picture signature is very significant, for the name of Abraham has far-reaching consequences in Judaism, Islam, and Christianity. In typical Egyptian art, the human offering is never clothed and is never shod in footwear. Similarly, the clothing on both the priest and Abraham is not characteristic of Egyptian art. Other changes include Abraham's hands, which are very un-Egyptian. Also, the bird's wings, which do not even match, are different from other facsimiles. They look more like hands than wings. (See "Egyptian wings and hands.") The representation of

Papyrus fragment

Portion of a painting of
Lucy Mack Smith

Abraham on the altar shows both hands up, which has not been found in any other papyri. It also shows, as Abraham declared, that he has been rescued, for he is no longer fastened to the altar. Another striking difference is that the female gender is not represented in this facsimile. In Egyptian hieroglyphs of this kind, at least one and often two females are always present. (See "Lion couch scenes" for comparisons.) However, with these changes or modifications, the facsimile better depicts concepts within the everlasting covenant: opposition in all things, the principles of obedience and sacrifice, and the principles of messengers and prophets of God.

There are two slightly different renderings of Facsimile No. 1 in possession of The Church of Jesus Christ of Latter-day Saints. One is the original fragment papyrus which was damaged along the fold and edges sometime after the Mormons had acquired it and is kept in the Church Historian's Office.[11] The second is a painting of Lucy Mack Smith which shows a rendering of the facsimile that was in the Mansion House hanging behind her. These two provide evidence of what the papyrus that Joseph worked with looked like.[12]

One can see minor changes in Facsimile No. 1 from the original fragment. (See "Papyrus fragment," "Portion of a painting of Lucy Mack Smith," and Facsimile No. 1.) These differences came about during the production of the blocks that Brother Reuben Hedlock

Egyptian knife

made under the direction of Joseph Smith for the printing of this facsimile. A quick comparison from papyrus to facsimile shows that the crocodile is slightly different, changing from a close replica of a crocodile in the papyrus to only a fair rendering of the animal in Facsimile No. 1. The knife is first the classic curve of the Egyptian and finally straight, or western in style. (See "Egyptian knife.") The head of the lion couch looks more like a lion on the papyrus, while in Facsimile No. 1, it appears more like a dog. Figure No. 8, one of the four canopic jars, goes from a distinguished man to a poor resemblance of a man. The priest of Pharaoh, Fig. 3, normally would always be drawn between Abraham and the lion couch so that the full body is visible, as Egyptian art dictates. Western art gives proper positioning precedence over body visibility. We see in this facsimile the proper positioning of the priest behind the table, blocking part of the body. Brother Hedlock's slight modifications towards a more western style do not altar the concepts of sacrifice, the conflict of good and evil, the manner of prayer, or the transmittal of powers from heaven to earth.

In summary, the culminating message of this facsimile is an illustration of the law of sacrifice, the powers of the priesthood, and messengers from heaven, while verifying that God knows each of His sons and daughters and has work for each to do within their agency and the ordinances of the everlasting covenant.

Figure 1: Messenger of God

Fig. 1—The Angel of the Lord.

Joseph Smith Jr. on numerous occasions defined an "angel" as a person who has a resurrected or translated body, even using Christ as an example, saying that after the Savior's death and resurrection, He was an angel when He received His body.[13] Using this definition of "angel" certainly gives greater understanding to the symbolism of Figure 1 when Joseph pronounces that it is "The Angel of the Lord." The scriptures teach that the spirit of God will teach a person what he must do to gain eternal life. "Every one that hearkeneth to the voice of the Spirit cometh unto God, even the Father. And the Father teacheth him of the covenant which he has renewed and confirmed upon you."[14]

The Book of Mormon explains, "And after God had appointed that these things should come unto man, behold, then he saw that it was expedient that man should know concerning the things whereof he had appointed unto them; Therefore he sent angels to converse with them, who caused men to behold of his glory."[15] In the very beginning, God established a pattern for communicating with His prophets through messengers. The first to be instructed in this manner was father Adam. Messengers have been the medium for imparting knowledge and giving direction to holy prophets through the ages since—to Adam, Enoch, Noah, Abraham, Moses, Isaiah, Ezekiel, Jeremiah, Lehi, Nephi, and Alma. Joseph Smith certainly understood this pattern after receiving over forty different messengers from heaven during his lifetime.[16] We have assurance that this means for delivering knowledge and giving help will always be available. The Prophet Malachi closed the Old Testament with this declaration: "The Lord's messenger shall prepare the way for the Second Coming."[17] The prophet Mormon described how these messengers work. "The office of their ministry is to call men … to fulfill and to do the work of the covenants of the Father … by declaring the word of Christ unto the chosen vessels of the Lord."[18]

Use of the figure of a hawk to symbolize an angel of the Lord that looks after members in covenant while they are in mortality is paramount in this facsimile. This same principle is illustrated in Figure 7 in Facsimile No. 2. In his narrative about the scene shown in Facsimile No. 1 Abraham speaks of "the angel of his presence"[19] and says, "Thou didst send thine angel to deliver me from the gods of Elkenah, and I will do well to hearken unto thy voice, therefore let thy servant rise up and depart in peace."[20] The apocryphal Book of the Revelation of Abraham reveals this angel as Iaoel. Abraham "heard the voice of the Holy One speaking: Go Iaoel, by the power of my unspeakable name, raise up this man for me, strengthen him, and quiet his trembling."[21] Dr. Nibley made this statement: "Joseph Smith was on very solid ground in identifying the hawk as the 'Angel of the Lord.' "[22] He also said Egyptians called it "the Messenger of Horus," "the Mediator," and "the Spirit of Light."[23] In Christianity, the dove has become the symbol of the Holy Ghost, and in many other cultures, a bird is used to symbolize a messenger of heaven. For example, the "thunderbird" to many American Indians is the initiator of all sounds and light of heaven.

To more clearly identify an angel-messenger to those of his seed, the hawk figure in Abraham's facsimile is modified from the Egyptian norm. The head is that of a bird. The body and wings look more like a human torso with arms and feet than the body and wings of a bird. The wing tips look much like the hand of Abraham as he is drawn on the couch. (See "Egyptian wings and hands" and compare to the wings in "Lion couch scenes.") The position of the bird is over Abraham's head and facing him. This is not consistent with Egyptian art. This bird image represents very well an angel-messenger of the Lord.

Figure 2: Abraham

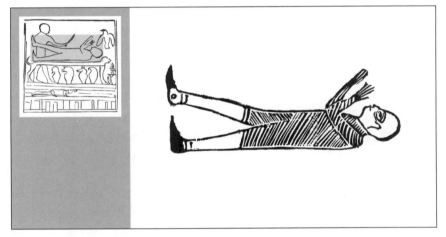

Fig. 2—Abraham fastened upon an altar.

This drawing depicts Abraham, a prophet of God, in peril of his life, petitioning the authorities of heaven for help. Symbolically, like Abraham, we are all on the altar of the world and need to petition God. On April 6, 1853, following the laying of the northeast cornerstone of the Salt Lake Temple by the Twelve Apostles, the Presidency of the Seventy, and the Presidency of the Elders' Quorum, Elder Parley P. Pratt gave possibly the greatest discourse ever given on this subject. It is fitting that this sermon was entitled "Spiritual Communication." He said, "If…we deny the philosophy or the fact of spiritual communication between the living and those who have died, we deny the very fountain from which emanated the great truths or principles which were the foundation of both the ancient and modern Church." He concluded with,

> And, moreover, the Lord has appointed a Holy Priesthood on the earth, and in the heavens, and also in the world of spirits; which Priesthood is after the order or similitude of His Son; and has committed to this Priesthood the keys of … correspondence or communication between angels, spirits, and men, and between all the holy departments, principalities, and powers of His government in all worlds.[24]

This facsimile, and specifically this figure, illustrates all of the probabilities of Elder Pratt's discourse.

Figure 2 illustrates that as a prophet, Abraham held the keys of the oracles of God,[25] a medium through which covenant mortals can knock, ask, seek, and will be recognized. This is the key of the "Right of Presidency" of the priesthood and is one of the great messages of the first facsimile. The keys of spiritual communication represent power and authority to converse with the Lord through the veil and to receive messengers according to individual needs. This was Joseph's understanding regarding keys enabling one to penetrate the veil when he said that Abraham had power to "talk and walk with God."[26] In this facsimile Abraham has revealed to the world a form of spiritual communication, one way to obtain the powers of heaven. "Let us lift up our heart with our hands unto God in the heavens."[27] What comfort to know that help is available to all worthy Saints. Abraham recorded: "And his voice was unto me: Abraham, Abraham, behold, my name is Jehovah, and I have heard thee, and have come down to deliver thee."[28] If the facsimile is turned on its side, one quickly recognizes what Brother Nibley has demonstrated: "He is praying…He is in the proper and conventional attitude of adoration—right foot thrust forward and hands raised before the face which is the correct depiction of supplication."[29] This specific position of prayer and adoration must have significance, for it is used extensively in the facsimiles, Holy Writ,[30] and among the shamans of Native Americans.

The principles of adoration and supplication are also depicted in Facsimile 2, Figures 23 and 24, where the baboons are shown in an upright stance with uplifted hands. This form of supplication is used to make an oath or covenant.[31] Joseph taught it at the School of the Prophets as part of a covenant salute to the brethren. "And he that cometh in and is faithful before me, and is a brother, or if they be brethren, they shall salute the president or teacher with uplifted hands to heaven, with this same prayer and covenant, or by saying Amen, in token of the same."[32]

Accounts from the Old Testament are numerous. Moses provides a great example of this posture's importance:

> And it came to pass, when Moses held up his hand, that Israel prevailed: and when he let down his hand, Amalek prevailed. But Moses' hands were heavy; and they took a stone, and put it under him, and he sat thereon; and Aaron and Hur stayed up his hands, the one on the one side, and the other on the other side; and his hands were steady until the going down of the sun.[33]

"And Solomon stood before the altar of the LORD in the presence of all the congregation of Israel, and spread forth his hands toward heaven."[34] "And Ezra blessed the LORD, the great God. And all the people answered, Amen, Amen, with lifting up their hands: and they bowed their heads, and worshiped the LORD with their faces to the ground."[35] In the New Testament the Savior himself followed this procedure. "And he led them out as far as to Bethany, and he lifted up his hands, and blessed them."[36]

In fact, in this dispensation the Lord has told us the reason to "organize yourselves" by building a temple was so "that your incomings may be in the name of the Lord; that your outgoings may be in the name of the Lord; that all your salutations may be in the name of the Lord, with uplifted hands unto the Most High."[37] In addition, the Psalmist indicated that the raising of one's hands is used as a sign that one is clean and pure before the Lord.[38] As the author of Job declared, "prepare thine heart, and stretch out thine hands toward him."[39]

It is an eternal truth that special spiritual powers of communication come through the ordinances in the everlasting covenant of Father, Son, and Holy Ghost. "Verily I say unto you, that ye are built upon my gospel; therefore ye shall call whatsoever things ye do call, in my name; therefore if ye call upon the Father, for the church, if it be in my name the Father will hear you."[40] Father Abraham used this facsimile to reveal to the world the very eternal objectives and divine purposes of the Gods—and how we might access them. Joseph Smith said, just three months before his death,

> Having a knowledge of God, we begin to know how to approach him, and how to ask so as to receive an answer. When we understand the character of God, and know how to come to him, he begins to unfold the heavens to us, and to tell us all about it. When we are ready to come to him, he is ready to come to us.[41]

The Book of Mormon describes specifics about penetrating the veil. "And because of the knowledge of this man [the brother of Jared] he could not be kept from beholding within the veil … Wherefore, having this perfect knowledge of God, he could not be kept from within the veil."[42] Is it any wonder that Brigham Young said,

> If you would take my counsel you never would cease to plead with the Lord, until He opened the eyes of your understanding and revealed eternity to you, that you might know for yourselves how things are, and when you know and keep in that spirit, you will never be deceived, but the spirit of truth will always be with you, and if you cleave to that, it will lead you into all truth and holiness.[43]

Figure 3: The Idolatrous Priest

Fig. 3 — The idolatrous priest of Elkenah attempting to offer up Abraham as a sacrifice.

This figure depicts two very important concepts: a false priest and idolatrous sacrifice. Abraham explains the practice of useless sacrifice among the people of Ur. "Therefore they turned their hearts to the sacrifice of the heathen in offering up their children unto these dumb idols, and hearkened not unto my voice, but endeavored to take away my life by the hand of the priest of Elkenah. The priest of Elkenah was also the priest of Pharaoh."[44] The individual in Figure 3 certainly is a representative of "the dark and benighted dominion of Sheol"[45] and the exact opposite of a prophet. Again, this is the old tale of opposition in all things.[46] Both father Abraham and Lucifer knew that "the whole mortal existence of man is neither more nor less than a preparatory state given to finite beings, a space wherein they may improve themselves for a higher state of being."[47] To accomplish this it "must needs be, that there is an opposition in all things. If not so ... righteousness could not be brought to pass, neither wickedness, neither holiness nor misery, neither good nor bad."[48]

The Book of Mormon relates what happened when their culture, as had Abraham's at this time, turned from God: "And it came to pass that there were sorceries, and witchcrafts, and magics; and the power of the evil one was wrought upon all the face of the land."[49] Abraham foresaw the eventual result of all such turning away:

> Behold, Potiphar's Hill was in the land of Ur, of Chaldea. And the Lord broke down the altar of Elkenah, and of the gods of the land, and utterly destroyed them, and smote the priest that he died; and there was great mourning in Chaldea, and also in the court of Pharaoh; which Pharaoh signifies king by royal blood.[50]

This figure illustrates much of what is going on in the world today; Gentiles are without the gift of the Holy Ghost and, therefore, without personal revelation. Revelation and the gift of the Holy Ghost are capstones within The Church of Jesus Christ of Latter-day Saints, and the ordinances of the everlasting covenant for both sides of the veil are the difference between the Lord's church and all other religions. The ordinances of the gospel are the difference between reaching the measure of one's creation and achieving a lesser kingdom. For it is through the ordinances that man can thwart the adversary and obtain the highest glory.[51] When plans to construct a new temple are announced, the jaws of hell gape open in an effort to block it, but like the idolatrous priest Elkenah, the idol gods and false priests of the land are quieted and "brought to nought."[52] God's temples will be built, and the ordinances of the everlasting covenant will be administered. The idolatrous priests of the world will be destroyed. The Gods of heaven are unchanging, and their words do stand.

Figure 4: Lion Couch

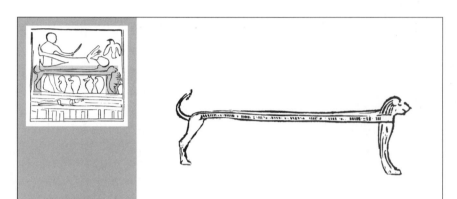

Fig. 4 —The altar for sacrifice by the idolatrous priests, standing before the gods of Elkenah, Libnah, Mahmackrah, Korash, and Pharaoh.

The fateful lion couch, with a sculptured lion's head upon it, is found everywhere in Egyptian art. (See "Lion couch scenes.") Joseph declared that this figure was "the altar for sacrifice." In Egypt, an altar, especially an altar of sacrifice, was usually in the form of a bed. Again we have here, reflected in one simple figure, a subject that is paramount within the plan of salvation. To be placed on a lion couch in Egypt would certainly be the ultimate example of being tried, tested, and proven in all things through the sacrifice of one's own life.

A true altar of God is fashioned after the heavenly altars.[53] One of the first things Adam and Eve did after being driven out of the Garden of Eden was to build an altar.[54] In the past there were altars "by the door of the tabernacle...of the congregation"[55] or "before the veil that is by the ark of the testimony before the mercy seat."[56] In the celestial kingdom stands "the golden altar which is before God."[57] A true altar represents a divine presence, heavenly messengers-angels of the Lord, a place for making and receiving covenants and offering up sacrifice, such as a broken heart and contrite spirit or even the sacrifice of personal sins.[58] It truly represents the meeting place where Deity accepts man's offerings.

Regarding sacrifice and trials, the Lord told Abraham, "And we will prove them herewith, to see if they will do all things whatsoever the Lord their God shall command them ... and they who keep their second estate shall have glory added upon their heads for ever and ever."[59] Later, using father Abraham as an example, the Lord said, "Therefore, they must needs be chastened and tried, even as Abraham, who was commanded to offer up his only son."[60] Jesus Christ has declared,

> And I give unto you a commandment, that ye shall forsake all evil and cleave unto all good, that ye shall live by every word which proceedeth forth out of the mouth of God ... and I will try you and prove you herewith. And whoso layeth down his life in my cause, for my name's sake, shall find it again, even life eternal.[61]

In the latter-days, the Lord said to Joseph, "And again, verily I say unto you ... that you may prove yourselves unto me that ye are faithful in all things whatsoever I command you, that I may bless you, and crown you with honor, immortality, and eternal life."[62] Joseph himself taught in the famous lectures on faith that "a religion that does not require the sacrifice of all things never has power sufficient to produce the faith necessary [to lead] unto life and salvation."[63] It brought joy to Joseph Smith when he was told by the Lord: "Behold, I have seen your sacrifices, and will forgive all your sins; I have seen your sacrifices in obedience to that which I have told you. Go, therefore, and I make a way for your escape, as I accepted the offering of Abraham of his son Isaac."[64] In our own day we have been told, "Therefore, be not afraid of your enemies, for I have decreed in my heart, saith the Lord, that I will prove you in all things, whether you will abide in my covenant, even unto death, that you may be found worthy."[65] This raises a question for the Saints of today. If sacrifice is such an important part of salvation, what are we going to lay upon the "Altar of Sacrifice?"

Figures 5–8: False Gods-Angels

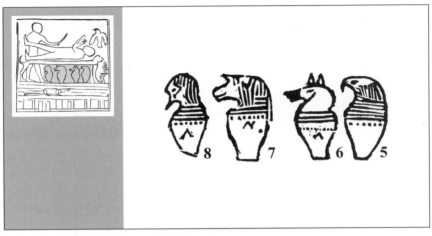

Fig. 5 — The idolatrous god of Elkenah.
Fig. 6 — The idolatrous god of Libnah.
Fig. 7 — The idolatrous god of Mahmackrah.
Fig. 8 — The idolatrous god of Korash.

This Egyptian motif is perfect for illustrating the concept of four entities with specific priesthood keys, even though in this facsimile they are represented by adulterous, idolatrous gods. (See Facsimile 2, Figure 6, in Chapter 6, representing four quarters of the earth.) In the Egyptian mind these figures represented deities of the entire earth, the four sons of Horus, each having a regional responsibility which encompassed, first, the four vital elements of the body, then the four quarters of this earth. (See "Artwork of the four entities.") The Apocalypse of Abraham and the Book of the Revelation of Abraham identify these four as having the faces of lion, man, ox, and eagle, though here we see them as Hawk, Jackal, Ape, and Man.[66] Each has specific functions and is associated with a name, body part, direction, god, color, and element:

Fig. 5—Hawk, Duametef-Cehhsonuf, stomach, East, Elkenah, red, water-time

Fig. 6—Jackal, Kebhsenef-Tuamutee, intestine, West, Libya, yellow, fire-energy

Fig. 7—Ape, Hapi-Mesta, lungs, North, Mahmackrah, white, air-space

Fig. 8—Man, Imset, liver, South, Korash, blue, earth-matter[67]

Authorities differ widely on what is ascribed to these four identities, and no two agree on all points. In addition, not one of the Egyptian mortuary temples hitherto excavated has provided an exact replica of the four figures found in other mortuaries.[68] We do know that in Egyptian theology the four canopic figures protect the body from harm and assist in its resurrection,[69] and they would have been numbered as above in the order of their importance.[70] We also know that these four entities, sometimes found as canopic jars, can and do stand for the earth and its four quarters, just as Joseph Smith said they did. To the Egyptians "the four quarters of the earth were people," and these figures have been demonstrated to represent segments of the earth.[71] After describing the bedstead, Abraham named the gods pictured beneath it, saying, "And it stood before the gods of Elkenah, Libnah, Mahmackrah, Korash, and also a god like unto that of Pharaoh, king of Egypt."[72] Even though Joseph in his explanation agreed, he also labeled them the gods of the Sun, Moon, Stars, and human industry (Man).[73] When pursued, this interpretation has much symbolic significance. The pronouncement that these are false idols is consistent with the use of the Egyptian canopic jars and shows how this motif with idolatrous gods is an illustration of opposition in all things.

Although the Prophet labeled these gods as idolatrous in this facsimile, we find the same four figures on the earth line of Facsimile No. 2, where they are specifically labeled as representing "this earth in its four quarters." This description is reminiscent of the Book of Revelation where the Apostle John talks of four angels over

Artwork of the four entities

the four quarters of the earth and tells us that they are the heavenly angels with sealing powers.[74] In modern scripture we are told that these four angels of God are they who give efficacy to the celestial marriage sealing of mortality and secure posterity to their parents.[75] The "Legends of Jews" identify three of these four angels as Raphael—the rescuer, angel of healing; Michael—angel

of prayer, mercy; and Gabriel—angel of war, angel of death, and
high priest of the heavenly temple.[76] (See Facsimile No. 2, Figure
6, and Appendix E, "Four Angels.") It is interesting, and probably
significant to the contention that Abraham was using these figures
to represent more than just false gods, that these four figures, even
though apostate, are facing to the right with Abraham, the lotus-
altar, and the hawk.

Figure 9: The False God

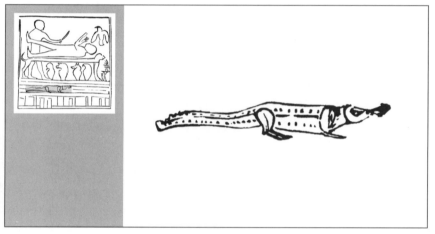

Fig. 9 —The idolatrous god of Pharaoh.

There were two modes of entry into Egypt, either by water or
by dessert. The guard of the water passage was the crocodile,
while that of the dessert was the Lion. Because of this the crocodile (Sobec) became an exclusive and primal protective god for the
Pharaoh, being loved or hated depending on the time and place
of history. Theologically, the crocodile "appears to Egyptians as a
mighty symbol of the resurrected Divine King."[77] It is symbolic
of the Pharaoh being able to consume the flesh and blood of
his victims, which refreshes and renews him through transfusion.

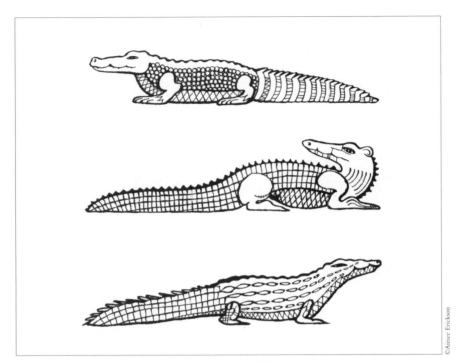

Egyptian crocodiles

The modified crocodile also signifies that this drawing is an altar of sacrifice, as a crocodile like this would never be found in an embalming scene. To see the face of the crocodile was to die. The crocodile here is uniquely and exactly what Joseph Smith called it, "the idolatrous god of Pharaoh."

Figure 10: Abraham in Egypt

Fig. 10—Abraham in Egypt.

What did Joseph notice that excited him so much when he first saw the scrolls ? Could he have come across or seen something during his translation of the Old Testament between March 1831 and July 1833 that he noticed again here? Could this drawing of an altar and lotus flower be what caused his excitement when he first saw the facsimiles? This lotus–altar signature of Abraham is on all three facsimiles. Had Joseph seen this drawing before and recognized it, or did father Abraham identify this to Joseph during one of his recorded appearances as representative of himself ?[78]

When the lotus flower is located "before the throne," it signifies that the event "takes place in Egypt."[79] In the Egyptian mind, the lotus represents the ultimate preservation and protects the living as well as the dead. It is also representative of the embodiment of ruling power. Brother Nibley has said that "the Egyptian lotus is as conspicuous in throne scenes from Palestine and Syria as it is in Egypt."[80] From his exposure to Egyptian hieroglyphs, Abraham was familiar with a signature motif, and what better symbol to represent one who literally holds the keys of eternal preservation and divine protection for his posterity. Certainly Joseph was right on the mark when he identified this symbol, for the set of symbols beneath the lotus flower is a signature identification of Abraham. It contains the symbol (,b) which is Ab, the symbol (r) for r, the symbol (h'n') for ha, and the symbol (m) for m, which altogether spell Abraham.[81] Hence the exactness of Joseph's explanation, as the name "Abraham" and the lotus of Egypt produce "Abraham in Egypt." There is even greater meaning than just identification in this symbol, however. By identifying himself, Abraham, a prophet and dispensation head, is telling the world that he sits here with great authority. Modern-day revelation describes this authority: "Behold, here is wisdom; yea, to be a seer, a revelator, a translator, and a prophet, having all the gifts of God which he bestows upon the head of the church."[82] The presentation of the name of Abraham has within it a greater connotation, even that of God, who said of Abraham that He would "put upon you my name, even the Priesthood of thy father, and my power shall be over thee ... through thy ministry my name shall be known in the earth forever, for I am thy God."[83]

The other part of this motif is the small sacrifice-altar formed within the symbol signature. In the Apocrypha, Abraham is told by the Lord that such a divine altar is associated with the temple of God.

> And he said: 'Hearken, Abraham, that which you see, the temple, the throne and the splendor signifies to me the Priesthood of the name of my glory, in which dwells every prayer of man, and in which is the rise of the kings and the prophets and as many sacrifices as I have determined shall be made among my people.[84]

The significance of the symbolism in this artistic signature becomes almost overwhelming. Abraham's entire life as a prophet of God was a wonderful example to the world of placing all that he had upon the altar. First himself, then his wife, and finally, his son. This figure alone, present in each facsimile, could very readily tie all of the divine truths within each facsimile together.

Figure 11: Pillars of Heaven

Fig. 11—Designed to represent the pillars of heaven as understood by the Egyptians.

It is interesting that this "pillar of heaven" design is used as the foundation of this facsimile. To the Egyptians, Pillars of Heaven represented doors or entrances to the various keys, powers, and blessings of Deity. The use of this drawing as the foundation reveals Abraham's personal understanding of what the source of all heavenly power is and where it comes from. A prophet of God knows that the foundation of the work is the power of God, which sustains and governs all within this universe of eternity as well as the eternities of the past and future. The first illustration of God's power in the form of pillars to this dispensation was conveyed in Joseph's account of the First Vision. "But, exerting all my powers to call upon God to deliver me out of the power of this enemy which had seized upon me . . . *I saw a pillar of light exactly over my head.*"[85] Bruce R. McConkie provided additional examples of this imagery when he likened pillars to the foundation of the plan of salvation.

> The three pillars of eternity, the three events, preeminent and transcendent above all others are the Creation, the Fall, and the Atonement. Every descendent of the posterity of Adam and Eve

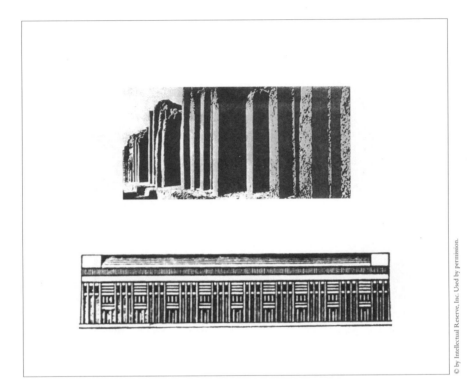

Egyptian doors and entrances

has been blessed by these pillars. They are the foundations upon which all things rest. Without any one of them, all things would lose their purpose and meaning, and the plans and designs of Deity would come to naught.[86]

The powers of the priesthood are not known by the gentile world today, but they were understood and imitated by the Pharaohs. This type of pillar entranceway is characteristic of Egyptian art and is found in almost all construction. What better way than pillar entrances or doors to convey access to the various powers and blessings of the everlasting covenant which have been made available to all mortals by our Godhead. (See "Egyptian doors and entrances.")

Figure 12: Expanse, Firmament, Heaven

Fig. 12—Raukeeyang, signifying expanse, or the firmament over our heads; but in this case, in relation to this subject, the Egyptians meant it to signify Shaumau, to be high, or the heavens, answering to the Hebrew word, Shaumahyeem.

Joseph's explanation of this figure is the same as Figure 4 of Facsimile No. 2. The best support for this drawing's representing firmament and the heavens comes first from Abraham, then other scriptures, and finally apocryphal writings. Abraham spoke of an expanse in his history of the Creation.

> And the Gods also said: Let there be an expanse in the midst of the waters ... And the Gods ordered the expanse ... And the Gods called the expanse, Heaven ... And organized them to be for lights in the expanse of the heaven to give light upon the earth; and it was so.[87]

Modern revelation also refers to the expanse of creation. "Thus saith the Lord your God, even Jesus Christ, the Great I AM, Alpha and Omega, the beginning and the end, the same which looked upon the wide expanse of eternity...before the world was made."[88] The apocryphal Abrahamic literature gives a revealing explanation—based on his own experiences—of expanse, firmament, and heaven.

> Behold the expanse under the plain upon which you now
> stand. There is no other in all space, save Him whom you have
> sought, and who loves you. And as he still spoke, behold the
> expanse opened itself, and below me the heavens ... And behold
> also upon this firmament was no other power except that of
> the seventh firmament, nor were there other shapes than the
> spiritual angels.[89]

The concept of the expanse or firmament of heaven shown in this
figure beautifully illustrates again the realms of the Gods and the
source of all power, even one eternal round from eternity to eternity, the ultimate fulfillment being, "Therefore if any man be in
Christ, he is a new creature: old things are passed away; behold, all
things are become new."[90]

This papyrus is a prophet's pictorial of gospel truths. It illustrates the
principles of covenant preparation, which necessitates understanding
the concepts of faith, priesthood, righteousness, obedience, sacrifice,
and prayer. These principles become efficacious in our lives through
the powers received from the ordinances of the everlasting covenant
established by God the Father, God the Redeemer, and God the
Testator as shown sequentially in Facsimiles 2 and 3.

Chapter 6:
Facsimile No. 2

acsimile No. 2 is often called by the scientific name *Hypo-cephalus*. The word comes from the Greek inscription *Hypo ten kephalen,* which means "under the head." The top part of a hypocephalus, that which is facing up in the circle, illustrates the powers of heaven, while the bottom half, that which is facing down, represents the mortal earth line.[1]

Facsimile 2 has been identified as the Hypocephalus of the Pharaoh Sheshonq (see Figure No. 8 of this facsimile) and contains within the top portion figures of heaven that represent different responsibilities and authority. The four images presented in Figures 1-4 depict four separate and distinct powers of the Gods. The images in Figures 2, 3, and 4, at the top of the facsimile, illustrate well the powers of the Godhead who entered into an everlasting covenant "according to Abraham's record." (See Chapter 3, "The Everlasting Covenant.") Oliver Cowdery must have been referring to these drawings when he wrote:

> The language in which this record is written is very comprehensive, and many of the hieroglyphics exceedingly striking. The evidence is apparent upon the face, that they were written by persons acquainted with the history of the creation,

Facsimile No. 2

Explanation (as given in the *Pearl of Great Price*):

Fig. 1   Kolob, signifying the first creation, nearest to the celestial, or the residence of God. First in government, the last pertaining to the measurement of time. The measurement according to celestial time, which celestial time signifies one day to a cubit. One day in Kolob is equal to a thousand years according to the measurement of this earth, which is called by the Egyptians Jah-oh-eh.

Fig. 2   Stands next to Kolob, called by the Egyptians Oliblish, which is the next grand governing creation near to the celestial or the place where God resides; holding the key of power also, pertaining to other planets; as revealed from God to Abraham, as he offered sacrifice upon an altar, which he had built unto the Lord.

Fig. 3   Is made to represent God, sitting upon his throne, clothed with power and authority; with a crown of eternal light upon his head; representing also the grand Key-words of the Holy Priesthood, as revealed to Adam in the Garden of Eden, as also to Seth, Noah, Melchizedek, Abraham, and all to whom the Priesthood was revealed.

Fig. 4   Answers to the Hebrew word Raukeeyang, signifying expanse, or the firmament of the heavens; also a numerical figure, in Egyptian signifying one thousand; answering to the measuring of the time of Oliblish, which is equal with Kolob in its revolution and in its measuring of time.

Fig. 5   Is called in Egyptian Enish-go-on-dosh; this is one of the governing planets also, and is said by the Egyptians to be the Sun, and to borrow its light from Kolob through the medium of Kae-e-vanrash, which is the grand Key, or, in other words, the governing power, which governs fifteen other fixed planets or stars, as also Floeese or the Moon, the Earth and the Sun in their annual revolutions. This planet receives its power through the medium of Kli-flos-is-es, or Hah-ko-kau-beam, the stars represented by numbers 22 and 23, receiving light from the revolutions of Kolob.

Fig. 6   Represents this earth in its four quarters.

Fig. 7   Represents God sitting upon his throne, revealing through the heavens the grand Key-words of the Priesthood; as, also, the sign of the Holy Ghost unto Abraham, in the form of a dove.

Fig. 8   Contains writings that cannot be revealed unto the world; but is to be had in the Holy Temple of God.

Fig. 9   Ought not to be revealed at the present time.

Fig. 10   Also.

Fig. 11   Also. If the world can find out these numbers, so let it be. Amen.

Figures 12, 13, 14, 15, 16, 17, 18, 19, 20, and 21 will be given in the own due time of the Lord.

the fall of man, and more or less of the correct ideas of notions of the Deity. The representation of the god-head—three, yet in one, is curiously drawn to give simply, though impressively, the writers views of that exalted personage.[2]

Scriptural testimonies to the three members of the Godhead are related in the Book of Mormon, first by the prophet Nephi and then by the Savior. Nephi, after speaking of the ordinances from "the gate" of "repentance and baptism" to "eternal life," said:

> And now, behold, my beloved brethren, this is the way; and there is none other way nor name given under heaven whereby man can be saved in the kingdom of God. And now, behold, this is the doctrine of Christ, and the only and true doctrine of the Father; and of the Son, and of the Holy Ghost, which is one God, without end. Amen.[3]

Jesus Christ explained this same concept in His first message to the Nephites at Bountiful when He said,

> Behold, verily, verily, I say unto you, I will declare unto you my doctrine. And this is my doctrine, and it is the doctrine which the Father hath given unto me; and I bear record of the Father, and the Father beareth record of me, and the Holy Ghost beareth record of the Father and me; and I bear record that the Father commandeth all men, everywhere, to repent and believe in me.[4]

This presentation of the Godhead, like the covenant they established, is everlasting, as it was "revealed to Adam in the Garden of Eden, as also to Seth, Noah, Melchizedek, Abraham, and all to whom the priesthood was revealed."[5] The scriptures make clear the necessity of understanding this concept: "And now, I would commend you to seek this Jesus ... that the grace of God the Father, and also the Lord Jesus Christ, and the Holy Ghost, which beareth record of them, may be and abide in you forever. Amen."[6] The last words Mormon wrote were "And may the grace of God the Father,

Bronze Hypocephali
(on site at Djed-hor Tomb at Abydos)

whose throne is high in the heavens, and our Lord Jesus Christ, who sitteth on the right hand of his power, until all things shall become subject unto him, be, and abide with you forever. Amen."[7] This is beautifully illustrated in this facsimile, which Abraham used with his non-Egyptian associates to convey ideas about God's work and glory.[8]

The hypocephalus finds its origins in the Book of the Dead in the chapter entitled "Chapter of Making Heat to Be under the Head of the Deceased." This chapter explains that by placing the knowledge contained on this disk under the head of a man, the body would retain its natural heat in the tomb. The instructions say the information should be "written upon a sheet of new papyrus and placed under the head of the deceased. Then great warmth shall be in every part of his body, even like that which was in him when he was upon earth."[9] We are informed that this power comes from the Cow-Goddess (Hathor) and Ra. Interestingly, Hathor and Ra are both depicted (Figures 5 and 7) on the earth line of this facsimile as potential gods. The practice of actually preparing the circular papyrus and placing it under the mummy's head came after Abraham's time. "The sheet was gummed on a piece of linen stiffened with plaster, and molded to the back of the head of the mummy in the coffin; trimmed into a circular form. It was intended to represent the Eye of Shu, or the Eye of Ra, or the Eye of Horus."[10] As time progressed, the small disk-shaped object was made of materials other than papyrus, such as stuccoed linen, bronze, wood, or clay.[11] (See "Bronze Hypocephali.")

This practice became common during the Twenty-sixth Dynasty (Princes of Sais, 663–525 B.C.) and continued until Christianity brought about its demise. Abraham lived in Egypt during the Twelfth Dynasty (ca. 1991–1786 B.C.), which raises the question of how the facsimile in the Book of Abraham could be attributed to Abraham. A review of written aids for the dead may help in understanding this apparent discrepancy.

From Egypt's earliest generations, aid to help the deceased attain the Field of Reeds (the Egyptian heaven) was deemed necessary. Recorded evidence of this notion goes back to around 3500 B.C. with records of oral promptings and utterances that became the foundation for the Pyramid Text, an aid written for the deceased. The first Pyramid Text hieroglyphs, which were actual writings to help the dead reach their goal, were found on the walls of burial chambers and anterooms. These were first used at the beginning of the Sixth Dynasty of the Old Kingdom (ca. 2345–2181 B.C.). Both the utterances and writings-prompters would have been in use for over four hundred years by the time Abraham and Sarah arrived in Egypt. Written instructions for the dead, copied on sheets of papyrus covered with magical texts, almost two hundred pages in number, became known as the Book of the Dead, which originated some five hundred years after Abraham. This would have been about the time of Moses, whose influence in Egypt came at the beginning of "The New Kingdom," the Eighteenth Dynasty (1567–1320 B.C.).

Another interesting point is that chapters 162–163 of the Book of the Dead contain information about hypocephali. These chapters are considered by some Egyptian scholars to be of foreign origin, or at least influenced by sources outside Egypt.[12] Could these outside influences have been prophets of the living God? We know that the first government of Egypt was established by the great-grandson of Noah and imitated the order established by father Adam.[13] A testimony of the imitation came when Abraham was instructed to take the gospel to Egypt,[14] and Joseph, son of Jacob, followed him, possibly arriving there in 1728 B.C.[15] These prophets had great political and spiritual influence among the early hierarchy of Egypt[16] which already had an inherent passion, even an obsession, with the afterlife.

The contents of the Egyptian hypocephali is a small resume or summary of all that has preceded it throughout the millennia of Egyptian history, the Pyramid Texts, Coffin Text, and the Book of the Dead.[17] It is very significant that the Pyramid Texts frequently mentioned a group of gods, even ascribing them to be "maker of mortals," "lord of the gods, god One" and "lord over heaven and earth."[18] The Egyptians ascribed to these gods many of the same qualities that we know to be true about members of the Godhead. One Egyptian belief that is abundantly illustrated is the pre-mortal life, showing the souls and spirits of men abiding in heaven with the gods.[19] From all this evidence, it seems that Pharaoh did a fine job of imitating much of the "order established by the fathers in the first generations."[20] With small changes, the hypocephali provided father Abraham an already existing source which he could use to represent the fullness of divine, sacred principles of the gospel of Jehovah inside a circle. Like all significant temple antiquities, various forms of the hypocephali are found in almost every culture. (See Appendix C, "Hypocephali.")

The heavenly top and the earthly bottom of all hypocephali are usually disproportionate, being closer to thirds than halves. The figures seen in Facsimile 2 are very consistent with other hypocephali, varying only slightly as to art and representation. The demographics of all true hypocephali are divided mathematically in segments of threes, totaling nine, with some segments departmentalized into four. The scenes presented in these segments vary as they convey different combinations of who, what, when, why, and how concerning powers, authority, stewardships, and responsibilities relating to both spiritual and mortal life. The various figures in the hypocephali always have intercourse and association one with another, illustrating beautifully the plan of salvation which of course incorporates both sides of the veil. Michael Lyon's research shows that the hypocephali—whether Greek, Oriental, or Egyptian in origin—is a symbol representing the sacred center of the universe.[21] The Church of Jesus Christ of Latter-day Saints teaches these same truths, and it is within the House of the Lord that ordinances are received which provide every blessing necessary to receive the fullness of this heavenly authority.

Facsimile 2, upper half

The upper half of Facsimile No. 2 shows individual entities that illustrate the powers of past, present, and future. One can see that the central, dominant figure of the upper half of a hypocephalus is Figure No. 1, representative of a two-headed deity. Mortals seek the eternal presence, the authority, the blessing, and the guidance of their God. It seemed important in every culture to become one with Deity by learning of God and becoming like

Him. This figure could illustrate all powers collectively, while Figures 2, 3, and 4 are presented to identify individually the powers of God the Creator, God the Redeemer, and God the Testator of the everlasting covenant. Remember, Oliver spoke of it as a "representation of the *god-head—three, yet in one.*" This power relationship of the "three Gods" may best be explained by what we know of their words. Bruce R. McConkie said,

> The words or deeds of either of them would be the words and deeds of the other in the same circumstance. Further, if a revelation comes from, or by the power of the Holy Ghost, ordinarily the words will be those of the Son, though what the Father would say, and the words may thus be considered as the Father's.[22]

(See "The Castillo," "Sacred altar with three panels" and "Native American sacred Ojibwa birch bark writings" in Chapter 3.) A scriptural example of this occurs when "the words of God" the Father were delivered by Jehovah in the first chapter of the Book of Moses in the Pearl of Great Price.[23]

The covenanted stewardship and power of each member of the Godhead is individual and unique. God the Creator is the Eternal Father, who created our spirits. It is He whom we worship and to whom all honor and glory is attributed. God the Redeemer, Jesus Christ, is He who justifies our sins to eternal law through the power of His atonement and opens the door that makes it possible to return into the presence of the Father through the power of an infinite resurrection. God the Testator, the Holy Ghost, sanctifies Saints by cleansing the individual and renewing his or her spirit from the effects of sin through His power. He dispenses knowledge and is the sealing testator of every covenant and ordinance that brings the efficacy of spiritual power to the individual. Figures 1 and 2 are represented to the viewers as individuals while explained as representing celestial bodies, using the same duality as "stars" for "spirits" found in Abraham chapter 3. The exception is Figure 3, where the drawing is that of an individual and the explanation says so. Figure 4 reverts back to showing a bird which the explana-

tion notes represents the attributes of heaven. Collectively these figures are representative of all powers of heaven as depicted through
Egyptian symbolism.

The plural term *gods* is found in the scriptures two hundred
and seventy-four times, with sixty-nine, or one-fifth, of that total
appearing in the Book of Abraham. The word is found thirty-two
times in chapter four alone—evidence that Abraham knew the
Gods, and he knew the Godhead. He knew of their perpetuation,
their laws, their creations, their stewardship, their councils, their
works, and their glories. Father Abraham represents the Gods in
both word and illustration. "And the Gods came down and formed
these the generations of the heavens and of the earth, when they
were formed in the day that the Gods formed the earth and the
heavens."[24] Through Abraham's words, Father in heaven, Elohim,
God the Creator, is the one asking the questions and making the
decisions: "Whom shall I send? ... And the Lord said: I will send
the first."[25] In Abraham's account it is Jehovah, God the Redeemer,
who answers: "And another answered and said: Here am I, send
me." In yet another scripture comes positive identification: "And
his voice was unto me: Abraham, Abraham, behold, my name is
Jehovah, and I have heard thee, and have come down to deliver
thee."[26] The explanation of Figure 3 states that this drawing "is
made to represent God, sitting upon his throne, clothed with power
and authority ... of the Holy Priesthood, as revealed to Adam." The
priesthood revealed to Adam was called after Jesus Christ, "the Holy
Priesthood, after the Order of the Son of God."[27]

Abraham is now a god, and the first twenty verses of the 132nd
section of the Doctrine and Covenants explain how one may
become a god through the ordinances and covenants of the everlasting covenant. President Lorenzo Snow wrote in May 1836: "I
formed the following couplet which expresses the revelation, as it
was shown to me, 'As man now is, God once was; As God now is,
man may be.'"[28] Joseph Smith described the process of becoming a
god as follows:

To inherit the same power, the same glory and the same exaltation, until you arrive at the station of a God, and ascend the throne of eternal power, the same as those who have gone before. What did Jesus do? 'Why; I do the things I saw my Father do when worlds came rolling into existence. My Father worked out his kingdom with fear and trembling, and I must do the same; and when I get my kingdom, I shall present it to my Father, so that he may obtain kingdom upon kingdom, and it will exalt him in glory. He will then take a higher exaltation, and I will take his place, and thereby become exalted myself.'[29]

Thus, the top half of Facsimile No. 2 illustrates the concept that is called the "Mysteries of Godliness."

Facsimile 2, lower half (inverted)

The lower half of this facsimile normally points downward (it has been inverted here) and illustrates the world below, or the mortality line.[30] Two genders that could comprise an eternal unit in mortality are illustrated symbolically in the lower half of this facsimile. From the beginning, the Egyptians included both genders when speaking of their god. The two genders contain the two powers and capacities represented here (male and female) which are necessary to become a god. Again we see the familiar dualism, as the explanation identifies Figure 5 as a celestial body, while the drawings are clearly those of a female and a cow. This female (Fig. 5) and

the male (Fig. 7), having separate responsibilities, are the key figures of this mortal
earth line. (See Appendix D, "Two Equal
Powers and Capacities.") As representatives
of creation and priesthood, they possess the
virtues of creation, all life, all power, and all
endurance, and may become the recipients
of heavenly blessings, both for mortality
and for the eternities to come. The earth
line is completed by Figure No. 6, made up
of four drawings in a row and then three
drawings on top of each other. The four
figures are described in Facsimile No. 1
and Figure 6 of this facsimile and enlarged
upon in Appendix E, "Angels of God." The

Chinese double helix

three drawings, a plant and a herbivorous and a carnivorous animal,
indicate that this line represents the mortal cycle of birth, life, and
death.

The figures on this earth line represent in a very wondrous way
all principles necessary to bring about the work and glory of the
Gods. While the absolute equality of male and female is eternal,
each works with a distinct authority and responsibility germane
to their eternal power and capacity. It is stated in "The Family: A
Proclamation to the World":

> All human beings—male and female—are created in the image
> of God. Each is a beloved spirit son or daughter of heavenly
> parents, and, as such, each has a divine nature and destiny.
> Gender is an essential characteristic of individual premortal,
> mortal, and eternal identity and purpose.[31]

(See "Chinese double helix" and "Father Sun, Mother Earth" for
examples of gender equality.)

All ordinances and commandments of the everlasting covenant lead
to the supernal sealing of two absolutely equal entities in marriage. In mortality the priesthood is conveyed only on sons, while

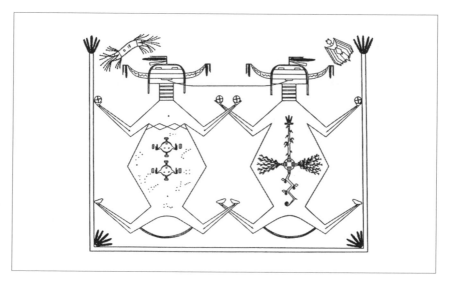

"Father Sun, Mother Earth,"
traditional Navajo sandpainting

in other ordinances some segments are specific to the responsibilities of each gender. Husband and wife each enter into the same covenants and enjoy the same blessings and power, for "in the ordinances thereof, the power of godliness is manifest."[32] Within the eternal unit each enjoys the authorities given them as royalty of their family. The husband, the king and priest, is the family head and God's representative through the powers of His Son's priesthood. The wife becomes a queen and priestess and may share the blessing or authority or power of her husband's priesthood within the patriarchal order of her own family.[33] Outside the temple, this patriarchal priesthood and authority operates only within the confines of the family kingdom, as it has done with all patriarchal fathers. This same order was followed by Abraham, Isaac, and Jacob. The primary purpose of the organization of the Church today is to preach the gospel and build up, support, and help perfect each family order on both sides of the veil. The Melchizedek (spiritual) Priesthood is first given to every male on both sides of the veil, and then the patriarchal order of that priesthood is put in place for every faithful couple at the time of their marriage for time and all eternity. The promise is given that ultimately husbands and wives will receive all that God can give them, all that Abraham, Isaac, and Jacob are now enjoying.[34] In the most simplistic interpretation of this facsimile, the fullness of heaven and earth, "one eternal round," is symbolized in a circle of prayer around the rim. It is only through the utilization of the powers illustrated that one can reach the full measure of their creation and receive the highest order of the celestial kingdom.[35] Those who are successful become the sons and daughters of God, through righteousness, and will bring glory and majesty to God.

The knowledge represented on this hypocephalus touches on the deeper mysteries of the gospel.

> Here then is eternal life—to know the only wise and true God. You have got to learn how to make yourselves Gods in order to save yourselves and be kings and priests to God. The same as all Gods have done—by going from a small capacity to a great capacity, from a small degree to another, from grace to grace, until the resurrection of the dead, from exaltation to exaltation—till you are able to sit in everlasting burnings and everlasting power and glory as those who have gone before, sit enthroned.[36]

Joseph Smith understood this mystery so well that he could have made the same statement about this facsimile that he made about the Book of Revelation: "The book of Revelation is one of the plainest books God ever caused to be written."[37] Joseph made obvious a great opportunity to temple recommend holders of The Church of Jesus Christ of Latter-day Saints when he wrote that much of the information on this facsimile cannot be revealed unto the world, but is to be understood and had in the holy temple of God.[38] The temple is a place where God the Testator, the Holy Ghost, can provide a full understanding of this facsimile. That is why temple attendance brings to pass the perfecting of the Saints; the transmittal of divine priesthood authority; and an explanation of prophets, priests, and kings, while making available to all the path necessary to obtain the fullness of the new and everlasting covenant, even the making of gods.

> For he that diligently seeketh shall find; and the mysteries of God shall be unfolded unto them, by the power of the Holy Ghost, as well in these times, as in times of old, and as well in times of old as in times to come; wherefore, the course of the Lord is one eternal round.[39]

The message of this facsimile is being clearly sent: "At that day ye shall know that I am in my Father, and ye in me, and I in you."[40]

Figure 1: Central Deity

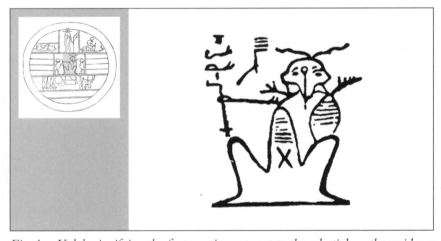

Fig. 1—Kolob, signifying the first creation, nearest to the celestial, or the residence of God. First in government, the last pertaining to the measurement of time. The measurement according to celestial time, which celestial time signifies one day to a cubit. One day in Kolob is equal to a thousand years according to the measurement of this earth, which is called by the Egyptians Jah-oh-eh.

This drawing is not only the central figure of the hypocephalus but, with Egyptian hieroglyphs, illustrates inherently and collectively all powers of heaven which the top half of the circle represents. The head and body top of this figure were missing on

Partial copy of Facsimile No. 2 from Church Historian's office

the original papyrus. In art, a blank area is called a lacunae. This blank area, or lacunae, has been illustrated as can be seen from the Church Historian's copy. (See "Partial copy of Facsimile No. 2 from Church Historian's office.") As you can see, the top of our Figure 1, along with Figure 3 and parts of numbers 2, 12, 13, 14, and 18 are missing. These areas were reconstructed by Reuben Hedlock under the supervision and with the approval of Joseph Smith the prophet, seer, and revelator.[41] The two heads found on Figure 1 are a distinct change from the Egyptian norm, which is usually four ram's heads. (See Appendix C, "Hypocephali.") In this drawing Joseph had only two identities placed where four are normally found. The male and female are a perfect illustration of the two necessary constituents of an eternal god. The two gender faces are also seen in Figure 2 as well as Figures 22 and 23. The representation of both genders seemed paramount in Egypt, as images of female and male are always drawn in the representation of dual heads. (See "Egyptian dual image art.") This knowledge was understood by the Egyptians

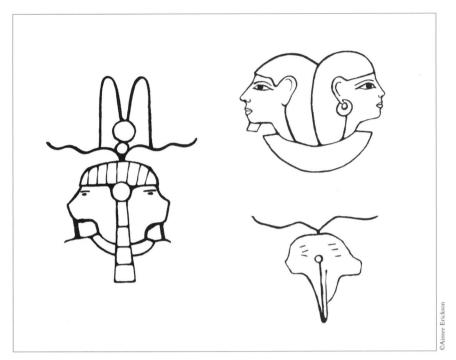

©Aimee Erickson

Egyptian dual image art

and seems to go back to the beginning; the first Egyptian dynasty depicted the first gods Ra and his consort Unas with Amen and his consort Ament as the primeval gods or king of the Gods.[42] Other paired gods representing both genders are Nau and Nen, Shu and Tefnut, and Tem and Temp.

While the explanation identifies this figure as a celestial body, the art shows a two-headed individual—dualism again. Joseph's explanation identifies the figure as a representation of "Kolob, signifying the first creation, nearest to the celestial, or the residence of God," and other explanations from Joseph in this facsimile relate back to the name *Kolob* as well. In speaking of this celestial body, Joseph said, "Kolob in the first degree...signifies the first great governing fixed star which is the farthest that ever has been discovered by the fathers which was discovered by Methusela and also by Abraham."[43] Joseph's statement provides the foundation for understanding the powers of the figures in 1, 2, 3, and 4. Figure 1's explanation informs us that Kolob represents that which is as far back as the fathers discovered. Joseph's explanation further explains this as representative of "the first creation," God's "residence," "first in government," and "the last pertaining to the measurement of time."

The prophet Joseph, in his great discourse just months before he died, shed more light on this. After speaking of the drama of the Creation and after explaining the word BERESHITH, Joseph said,

> Where did it come from? When the inspired man wrote it, he did not put the first part—the BE—there; but a man—an old Jew without any authority—put it there. He thought it too bad to begin to talk about the head of any man. It read in the first: 'The Head One of the Gods brought forth the Gods.' This is the true meaning of the words. ROSHITH (BARA ELOHIM) signifies (the Head) to bring forth the Elohim ... Thus, the Head God brought forth the Head Gods in the grand, head council.[44]

Joseph's two statements together may help one understand his explanation of Figure 1: "Kolob, signifying the first creation." Could the first creation be descriptive of the sphere of the Gods, the realm of the patriarchal order of exalted fathers and mothers? Hence the saying, "For do we not read that God is the same yesterday, today, and forever, and in him there is no variableness neither shadow of changing?"[45] Joseph Smith's explanation of this figure also says, "first in government, last in measurement of time." This part of Joseph's statement seems to describe well "a council of the gods" working within the sphere of the Gods or the "patriarchal order of exalted fathers" which Joseph referred to in the same King Follett Sermon.[46] Remember, on seeing the scrolls for the first time, Oliver Cowdery said, "The representation of the Godhead—three yet in one."[47] This statement is genesis testimony that Figure 1 could be the multiple representation of the Gods that Oliver is making reference to.

It is also in this motif that the two baboons, one on each side of Figure 1, are showing honor and thereby giving power to the figure. It is significant that this honor and supplication is shown in this figure, the one that may illustrate the source of all powers 'the sphere of the gods." (See Figures 22 and 23.) Joseph said Figure 1 "receives its power through the medium" of the two figures showing honor with uplifted hands. This figure certainly seems the best one in which to illustrate this concept. The scriptures teach that Deity's power comes from the honor of their children who are obedient and reach the measure of their creation. In the well-known story of a disobedient son who wanted his father's honor-power, the scriptures say, "For, behold, the devil was before Adam, for he rebelled against me, saying, Give me thine honor, which is my power"[48] and "Wherefore, because that Satan rebelled against me [instead of honoring God], and sought to destroy the agency of man ... and also, that I should give unto him mine own power ... I caused that he should be cast down."[49]

The male entity of this dual-faced figure is holding a scepter in his right hand which represents the supreme symbols of life, dominion, and stability—the virtues of creation and, collectively, the power of the council of the Gods. The three hieroglyphic ideograms making up this scepter are the Anh (pronounced Ankh), the Djed-column, and the Was (wsr) scepter. (See "Ankh symbol, Djed-column, and Was scepter.") Under Joseph's prophetic mantel, a very unique modification was made. Notice that the powers of this scepter are different from the three (in one) ideograms that are clearly seen on the left knee (and sometimes both knees in other Egyptian hypocephali). Notice that there is just one symbol, the Was scep-ter, in the Henry Meux Hypocephalus in Appendix C, and only the one Djed-column on the Church Historian's partial copy, both seemingly on the left knee. (See Appendix C, "Hypocephali.") The change to these three separate ideograms in the right hand from the Egyptian norm is again indicative of that which is being illustrated. First, the three powers are individual and distinct, and second, they are found in the right hand. The right hand is the hand involved in every significant event of all sacred ordinances of the everlasting

Ankh symbol, Djed-column, and Was scepter

covenant. What Dr. Nibley said concerning this scepter seems to confirm that the power illustrated in this figure is representative of the council of the Gods. He said, "His royal scepter denotes both the begetter as well as the King of Kings."[50]

This Wsr scepter of divine judgment is symbolic of "life-giving power" and later "of well being and happiness . . . and posterity."[51] The Ankh symbol represents life not only in the Egyptian language but also in Greek and Coptic. As "an imperishable vital force the ankh was used on temple walls, stelae and elsewhere. As a symbol, it points to divine, eternal, existence,"[52] prolonged life for the living and resurrection for the dead. The gods always carried it because it represented not only the power of life, but immortality and all dominion. The significance of the Djed (dt) column, Djed-pillar, has never really been explained. Every scholar seems to approach its significance from a different direction; however, in Egyptology, it has come to have a well-accepted meaning as a column of durability, the representation of God's backbone, encompassing stability, health, happiness, and peace. The summation of these three ideograms was often shortened to having all power, all life, and all stability, which is certainly indicative of composite Deities. The illustrations of this figure brings to mind the scripture, "That the rights of the priesthood are inseparably connected with the powers of heaven."[53] The horns on top of the heads are a beautiful and simple representation of power, maybe even ultimate power or the source of all power.

The drawing of the left or female side of the body, as well as the ideograms extending from both shoulders, lead one to speculation. The left side may represent part of the torso because of the position of the head, while the shoulder insignias are probably jackal heads. Jackals are tomb robbers that dig and bring the body out of the grave to a new life; hence, they are representative of another source of infinite power. See Figure 2 for a better delineated drawing of the jackal sign on the shoulders.

Figure 2: God the Creator

Fig. 2—Stands next to Kolob, called by the Egyptians Oliblish, which is the next grand governing creation near to the celestial or the place where God resides; holding the key of power also, pertaining to other planets; as revealed from God to Abraham, as he offered sacrifice upon an altar, which he had built unto the Lord.

Figure 2 is the center of the three figures that strike across the top of the hypocephalus, which represents the heavens above. This profound middle drawing represents all of the attributes and powers of God the Creator, He whom we worship. First it may be seen that the top part of Figure 2 is a mirror facial image of Figure 1. In Figure 2, the male face is on the right side, while in Figure 1 it is on the left side. The scepter of power and authority is different, but is also held by the male in this mirror image of Figure 1. The mirror image concept is significant, for it supports Joseph's placing a two-faced deity here instead of the normal Egyptian four-faced deity. The mirror image of Father and Son was described by Joseph when he said, I "saw two glorious personages, who exactly resembled each other in features and likeness."[54] Holy Writ gives this illustration: "Then answered Jesus and said unto them, Verily, verily, I say unto you, the Son can do nothing of himself, but what he seeth the Father do: for what things soever he doeth, these also doeth the Son likewise."[55] When the Savior was among the Jews, He did not identify himself as being perfect or a mirror image of the Father, for He had not yet completed His part of the covenant.[56] Upon completion of His covenant with the Father and the Holy Ghost through His atonement and resurrection, the Savior achieved the mirror image. This was confirmed when He addressed the Nephites. "Therefore I would that ye should be perfect even as I, or your Father who is in heaven is perfect."[57] This type of perfection means to complete or finish our individual covenants so that our image may be like that of the Godhead. After the fulfillment of Jehovah's atonement and resurrection He asked those present, "What manner of men ought ye to be? Verily I say unto you, even as I am."[58] After the ancient Nephites had begun the transition towards the image of Christ, the Lord told them,

> Blessed are ye because of your faith. And now behold, my joy is full. And when he had said these words, he wept ... he who had descended below all things, the Man of Sorrows, he who bore all our griefs. The height of his infinite capacity for joy is the inverse, mirror image of the depth of his capacity to bear our burdens.[59]

Joseph, in his explanation of Figure 2, again provides a dualistic interpretation by describing heavenly creations represented by Abraham's drawings of a two-headed individual. Joseph's description, like Abraham's drawing, is representative of God the Creator. Joseph's explanation reads: "Stands next to Kolob, called by the Egyptians Oliblish." Is not the eternal God under the direction of eternal Gods, from eternity to eternity? Does not God reside as an exalted being among the exalted Fathers which make up the grand union of divine minds for this eternity?[60] (See Appendix F, "An Eternity.") In his research, Dr. Nibley made a tremendous analogy of this figure to our "Most High God," our Father in heaven. He said, "Figure 2 on a Hypocephalus says 'I am he who closes and he who opens and I am but one.' He is the moment at which past and future meet, looking both to yesterday and tomorrow.'"[61] We receive further enlightenment from Abraham:

> Howbeit that he made the greater star; as, also, if there be two spirits, and one shall be more intelligent than the other, yet these two spirits, notwithstanding one is more intelligent than the other, have no beginning; they existed before, they shall have no end, they shall exist after, for they are gnolaum, or eternal.[62]

Now the challenge is to determine which of Abraham's next five verses are spoken by Elohim and which are spoken by Jehovah. We are told in scripture that God the Creator, God the Redeemer, and God the Testator speak as one, but it would be interesting to know the identity of the speaker in this instance.

The lower right corner of the papyrus Joseph had in his possession, which now contains this figure, was blank, part of the lacunae. (See "Partial copy of Facsimile No. 2 from Church Historian's office.") Joseph's restoration of the lacunae contains the very significant lotus offering table-altar symbol of Abraham. Its presence here is unique from any other Egyptian hypocephalus. This lotus altar signature is a testimony to the concept that Facsimile No. 2 in general and Figure 2 specifically deal with Abraham's covenant dispensation, the keys of which were restored to our dispensation in the Kirtland Temple.

Its placement here also conveys that it was Abraham who entered into covenant with "God the Creator" (which "in pure language spoken by Adam...is Ahman," which in turn is very similar to "the Egyptian deity Ammon, or Amon or Amen,"[63] the God to which all petitions were made). One can see that the rest of Figure 2 is very distinguishable in the original papyrus.

Figure 2 would be described by an Egyptologist as "a two-headed deity wearing the double-plumed crown of Amen, with ram's horns mounted on it. On his shoulders are jackal heads and he is holding the jackal standard of Wepwawet. Also to his right is a line of hieroglyphics 'The name of this Mighty God.' "[64] The staff is a wooden key that opens the womb and other worlds. The (male and female) powers-capacities-responsibilities incorporated in Deity are defined by Joseph as "holding the key of power." Keys, the governing right of the presidency of the priesthood, certainly would apply to the patriarchal order of an eternal unit inherent to the Almighty Father in heaven. The prophet Joseph said, "For all the ordinances and duties that ever have been required by the priesthood, under the directions and commandments of the Almighty in any of the dispensations, shall all be had in the last dispensation."[65]

In Church doctrine, a figure of this power would represent the Almighty, "God the Creator," Elohim the Eternal Father[66] of our spirit bodies. We are His spirit children. He is an exalted Man in the most literal terms. He is a glorified, exalted, resurrected being. He is a Holy Man. He is Ahman, the Almighty Elohim. He is omnipotent (has unlimited power) and omniscient (knows all things) relative to the universe in which mortals live and is himself the source and possessor of all true power manifest in it. This is part of what it means to be exalted. This is why we, His children, may safely put our faith and trust in Him as an exalted being with whom we can talk as one man talks with another. We worship and pray to the Father and offer all other sacred performances to Him in the name of the Son, Jesus Christ. Charles W. Penrose said concerning this, "The person whom I worship I acknowledge as my Father. Through Him I may learn to understand the secrets and mysteries of eternity, those things that never had a beginning and will never have an end."[67] Joseph Smith summarized it this way:

> I will refute that idea and take away the veil so you may see. Truth is the touchstone. These things are incomprehensible to some, but they are simple. The first principle of truth and of the Gospel is to know for a certainty the character of God, and that we may converse with Him the same as one man with another, and that He once was a man like one of us and that God Himself, the Father of us all, once dwelled on an earth the same as Jesus Christ did in the flesh and like us ... God himself was once as we are now, and is an exalted man, and sits enthroned in yonder heavens! That is the great secret.[68]

Figure 3: God the Redeemer

Fig. 3—Is made to represent God, sitting upon his throne, clothed with power and authority; with a crown of eternal light upon his head; representing also the grand Key-words of the Holy Priesthood, as revealed to Adam in the Garden of Eden, as also to Seth, Noah, Melchizedek, Abraham, and all to whom the Priesthood was revealed.

Joseph's explanation for this figure is different from the other figures on this hypocephalus, as it speaks only of God and not celestial bodies. This explanation seems to be almost verbatim from wordage in the Doctrine and Covenants. This area of the facsimile was also part of the lacunae and had to be filled in. (See "Partial copy of Facsimile No. 2 from Church Historian's office.") As he was directed by the prophet Joseph, Brother Reuben Hedlock, the artist scribe, put in Figure 3. This would have been, for Joseph, like translating the Book of Mormon and correcting the Old and New Testaments with scribes through the power of God. In doing so he certainly would have received personal knowledge of the representation that needed to be re-created.

IV Frame [Trinity] Papyrus

During the process of restoring Figure 3, Joseph, either by revelation or the direction of father Abraham, used the papyrus fragment No. IV called the "Framed Trinity Papyrus,"[69] which Joseph had in his possession.[70] (See "IV Frame [Trinity] Papyrus.") One can see that the Frame IV and Figure 3 are almost identical. It can be seen that there is only one individual in Figure 3, while the Egyptian Re in Solar Barks always illustrates more than one individual. (See "Re in solar bark.") The presence of two or more persons is almost always found in this type of Egyptian art.

The fact that here there is only one reminds us that the Lord was alone in the winepress, and, as the Son of God, Christ is the only advocate with the Father. Under the Father's empowerment, the great I Am is the creator of the heavens and earth. He is the Christ.

Re in solar bark

"Jesus saith ... I am the way, the truth, and the life: no man cometh unto the Father, but by me."[71] These powers are represented well by the staff being held here, which is different from the staffs held in Figures 1 and 2. The staff here is the single Was (w3s) scepter, symbol of power, judgment, and "life-giving power." Joseph reflects this in his explanation: "a god sitting on his throne clothed with power and authority." The first principle of the gospel is "faith in the Lord Jesus Christ." The gospel is so defined by Christ himself: "And this is my gospel which I have given unto you—that I came into the world to do the will of my Father, because my Father sent me. And my Father sent me that I might be lifted up upon the cross ... that I might draw all men unto me."[72] Indeed, the Atonement is the gospel. Just as the creative and redemptive power of Christ extends to the earth and all things thereon, it is also infinite in its reach to the expanse of worlds beyond this, with the power of the resurrection being universal in scope.[73] This is the god to whom every knee must bow and every tongue confess that He is the Christ.

The most precious of all gifts is to know that Jesus is the Christ, His being the only name given under heaven as a medium through which mortals can approach God. He is the mediator of the new covenant.[74] To redeem necessitates power. The Savior told His disciples, following His atonement and resurrection, "All power is given unto me in heaven and in earth."[75] This same Jehovah spoke to Moses, saying, "I am the God of thy father, the God of Abraham, the God of Isaac, and the God of Jacob. And Moses hid his face; for he was afraid to look upon God."[76] The Book of Mormon is full of such scriptures. "But behold, I will show unto you a God of miracles, even the God of Abraham, and the God of Isaac, and the God of Jacob; and it is that same God who created the heavens and the earth, and all things that in them are."[77] "Behold, I am he that gave the law, and I am he who covenanted with my people Israel; therefore, the law in me is fulfilled, for I have come to fulfil the law; therefore it hath an end."[78] To the brother of Jared the Lord said,

> Behold, I am he who was prepared from the foundation of the world to redeem my people. Behold, I am Jesus Christ. I am the Father and the Son. In me shall all mankind have life, and that eternally, even they who shall believe on my name; and they shall become my sons and my daughters.[79]

The June 30, 1916, Doctrinal Exposition by the First Presidency and the Twelve verifies that the Savior is the "Father" by virtue of His creating heaven and earth, is the "Father" of those who abide in His gospel, and is the "Father" by divine investiture of authority. The New Testament carries the Savior's testimony of himself: "Jesus said unto them, Verily, verily, I say unto you, Before Abraham was, I am."[80] The Doctrine and Covenants declares, "Thus saith the Lord your God, even Jesus Christ, the Great I AM, Alpha and Omega, the beginning and the end, the same which looked upon the wide expanse of eternity, and all the seraphic hosts of heaven, before the world was made."[81] It is the Savior's "all power," the atonement and the resurrection, that allows one to gain access back into the fullness of Father in heaven.[82]

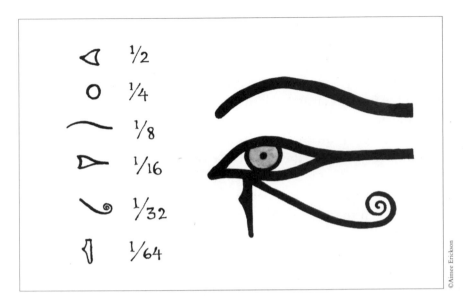

Utchat [Wedjat] eye and chart

Figure 3 represents the powers that have been given to His representatives on earth in every dispensation. Abraham knew that he was an instrument unto the Lord to use all of the authority Figure 3 illustrates.[83] President John Taylor said this authority

> is to hold the keys of all the spiritual blessings of the Church; to have the privilege of receiving the mysteries of the kingdom of heaven, to have the heavens open to them, to commune with the general assembly; and Church of the Firstborn and to enjoy the communion and presence of God the Father, and Jesus the mediator of the new covenant, and to preside over all the spiritual officers of the Church.[84]

Egyptian theology refers to Figure 3 as God Ra, the sun-god, the creator of gods and men. Notice this figure has a very well-pronounced circle in front of the head. Normally the sun disk is on top of the head. (See Appendix C, "Hypocephali.") Joseph refers to it as a "crown of eternal light upon his head." Is not Jesus Christ the source of light? Scriptures testify that "God is light," the source of all light, the everlasting light.[85] A plain circle is emblematic of a white stone given to the righteous in many cultures. All standard works speak of the white stone. "And a white stone is given to each of those who come into the celestial kingdom, whereon is a new name written, which no man knoweth save he that receiveth it. The new name is the key word"[86] (Joseph describes this figure as "representing also the grand Key-words of the Holy Priesthood."). Even today, in secular coronations, the union of a king or queen with their kingdom is often symbolized between the sovereign and a stone. This sun disk, crown of eternal light or key word, is well defined by the pseudepigraphal Book of Third Enoch:

> His radiance like the light of the morning star, his image like the greater light ... The sapphire stone on his head is the size of the whole world and like the brilliance of the heavens themselves in clarity ... The crown on his head is radiant like the throne of glory ... There is no kind of radiance, no kind of splendor, no kind of brilliance, no kind of light in the world which is not placed in that crown ... and the name of the crown on his head is 'Prince of Peace.'[87]

Jesus Christ is the prince of peace.

Figure 3 also includes two Utchat (Wedjat) Eyes, one in front and one behind the figure. This symbol represents light, protection, perfection, and the source of all health and happiness. Abraham knew that these depict some of the blessing of the Savior. The Egyptians celebrate a great festival on the longest day of the Egyptian year in honor of the "filling of the Utchat."[88] Those involved, surrounding twelve altars, sing praises to God. These praises are very similar to the "Song of Redeeming Love" found in all four standard works of the Church.[89] Like Figure 3, two Egyptian Utchats, one facing to the right and the other to the left, represent the sun and the moon and the halves of the sun's daily course, where the living are under the protection of he who controls all power.[90] Certainly this is all indicative of the Lord Jesus Christ. (See "Utchat [Wedjat] eye and chart.") Also found in this figure is the lotus blossom offering table, symbolic of rebirth and signifying a witness to the redemptive mission of the Savior. This figure is also seated on the Solar Bark,

Solar barks

which represents Re's sun journey across the sky on the waters of Nun. This is a second witness symbolizing resurrection and rebirth on an exalted platform that carries one to heaven. What better representation of the infinite redemptive powers provided by "God the Redeemer" of the everlasting covenant. (See "Solar barks.")

All powers shown in this figure are available through the Redeemer to every worthy member of the Church as they enter into the ordinances and covenants of the everlasting covenant. All is accomplished by those holding the same priesthood after the Son of God who is Christ the Redeemer. Joseph Smith's translation of Genesis 14 says,

> For God having sworn unto Enoch and unto his seed with an oath by himself; that every one being ordained after this order and calling should have power, by faith, to break mountains, to divide the seas, to dry up waters, to turn them out of their course; to put at defiance the armies of nations, to divide the earth, to break every band, to stand in the presence of God; to do all things according to his will, according to his command, subdue principalities and powers; and this by the will of the Son of God which was from before the foundation of the world.[91]

The Apostle Paul said, "For ye are all the children of God by faith in Christ Jesus...ye are all one in Christ Jesus. And if ye be Christ's, then are ye Abraham's seed, and heirs according to the promise."[92]

The great message here then is to become like the god of eternal life. This was the same goal which the Egyptians desired. The Savior said, "Behold, I am the law, and the light. Look unto me, and endure to the end, and ye shall live; for unto him that endureth to the end will I give eternal life."[93] The things shown in this figure certainly illustrate all of these attributes and powers of Jehovah, the Lord and Savior Jesus Christ.

Figure 4: God the Testator

Fig. 4—Answers to the Hebrew word Raukeeyang, signifying expanse, or the firmament of the heavens; also a numerical figure, in Egyptian signifying one thousand; answering to the measuring of the time of Oliblish, which is equal with Kolob in its revolution and in its measuring of time.

Figure 4 shows a hawk with outspread wings seated upon a boat moving through the heavens. The hawk is one of the most familiar figures in Egyptian hieroglyphs, and this scene is found in most hypocephali. In Egyptology the hawk can represent many gods and powers, but usually it represents the two gods Sokar and Horus. The hawk's duties usually have to do with the well-being of the body or soul. The outspread wings are not normally found when representing Egyptian gods; however, with extended wings, the hawk becomes a good symbol to illustrate expansion, heavenly truth, and power. The boat the hawk is sitting in is moving through the universe. Again this is indicative of Joseph Smith's explanatory comment on the "expanse" or "firmament of the heavens," which the medium of the Holy Ghost fills. Joseph said the bird in Figure 7 "is the sign of the Holy Ghost to Abraham," certainly a testament to the bird representing "God the Testator."

Joseph's explanation of this figure is similar to that of Figure 12 of Facsimile No. 1. Both signify expanse or the firmament of the heavens (Egyptian Shaumau and Hebrew Shaumahyeem). So Joseph's use of "expanse" or "firmament of heaven" to describe the domain of the Holy Spirit is represented well, while the art of the barge and hawk with outstretched wings provides a good symbol of His accessibility. The Book of Mormon tells us, "For behold, again I say unto you that if ye will enter in by the way, and receive the Holy Ghost, it will show unto you all things what ye should do."[94] This would seem to illustrate the availability to all who diligently seek. "For he that diligently seeketh shall find; and the mysteries of God shall be unfolded unto them, by the power of the Holy Ghost ... wherefore, the course of the Lord is one eternal round."[95] In the apocryphal Book of the Revelation of Abraham we are told, "I am called Laoel by him who shaketh the creations of the firmament to the breadth of the seventh heaven, power being vested in me through his unspeakable name."[96] Church doctrine tells us that "the Holy Ghost by reason of his universally diffused, subtle and powerful influence, is the medium through which the Godhead operates to create acts and governmental functions."[97] We know "this Holy Spirit, under the control of the Great Elohim, is the grand moving cause of all Intelligences, and by which they act" and

> is the controlling agent or executive, which organizes and puts in motion all worlds, and which, by the mandate of the Almighty, or of any of His commissioned agents, performs all the mighty wonders, signs and miracles, ever manifested in the name of the Lord ... It penetrates the pores of the most solid substances, pierces the human system to its most inward

recesses, discerns the thoughts and intents of the heart. It has power to move through space with inconceivable velocity, far exceeding the tardy motions of electricity or physical light.[98]

We know that "His influence quickens all the intellectual faculties, increases, enlarges, expands and purifies all the natural passions and affections; and adapts them by the gift of wisdom to their lawful use."[99]

The Holy Ghost is a personage of spirit, not possessing a body of flesh and bone, but "is capable of manifesting himself in the form of a man."[100] His mission is to dwell, figuratively, in the faithful and to speak to their spirits in a special and particular way, even spirit to spirit, which can be done because He himself is a spirit. The gift of the Holy Ghost is the right to have the companionship of the Holy Ghost. Joseph, in his great King Follett discourse, explained that

> all things whatsoever God in His infinite reason has seen fit and proper to reveal to us, while we are dwelling in our mortal state, in regard to our mortal bodies, are revealed to us in the abstract and independent of affinity of this mortal tabernacle. His commandments are revealed to our spirits precisely the same as though we had no bodies at all and those revelations which must of necessity save our spirits will save our bodies. God reveals them to us in the view of no eternal dissolution of our bodily tabernacles.[101]

"The power of the Holy Ghost then is the spirit of prophecy and revelation; His office is that of enlightenment of the mind, quickening of the intellect, and sanctification of the soul," states James E. Talmage.[102] If members of the Church really understood all of this, one might say "forty days and forty nights I ate no bread and drank no water, for the sight of the angel who was with me was my bread, and his speech was my drink."[103]

Through the commandments, laws, and ordinances of the everlasting covenant, we can achieve constant companionship with the Holy Spirit. When this happens the individual can better develop spiritual gifts and obtain greater spiritual attributes, being filled with the fruits of the Holy Ghost.[104] Eternal blessings then follow, as witnessed in the great declaration, "The Holy Ghost shall be thy constant companion, and thy scepter an unchanging scepter of righteousness and truth; and thy dominion shall be an everlasting dominion, and without compulsory means it shall flow unto thee forever and ever."[105]

We may summarize all of the above by saying that God the Testator, the Holy Ghost or Holy Spirit, is the agent, means, or influence by which the will, power, and intelligence of the Godhead is transmitted throughout space. It is the spirit of intelligence that permeates the universe and gives understanding to the spirits of men, the grand moving cause by which all faith, righteousness, and virtue performs. God the third, the witness or Testator, would truly represent well He "who sitteth upon his throne, who is in the bosom of eternity, who is in the midst of all things."[106] Joseph said that the

> Holy Ghost has no other effect than pure intelligence. It is more powerful in expanding the mind, enlightening the understanding, and storing the intellect with present knowledge of a man who is of the literal seed of Abraham, than one that is a Gentile. For as the Holy Ghost falls upon one of the literal seed of Abraham, it is calm and serene: and his whole soul and body are only exercised by the pure spirit of intelligence.[107]

This ancient papyrus figure represents this doctrine very well.

Figure 5: Mother of Life

Fig. 5—Is called in Egyptian Enish-go-on-dosh; this is one of the governing planets also, and is said by the Egyptians to be the Sun, and to borrow its light from Kolob through the medium of Kae-e-vanrash, which is the grand Key, or, in other words, the governing power, which governs fifteen other fixed planets or stars, as also Floeese or the Moon, the Earth and the Sun in their annual revolutions. This planet receives its power through the medium of Kli-flos-is-es, or Hah-ko-kau-beam, the stars represented by numbers 22 and 23, receiving light from the revolutions of Kolob.

The explanation of this figure again incorporates the dual concepts of celestial bodies and individuals. Joseph speaks of planets and astronomical principles, and Abraham depicts two figures representing Hathor. Of all the Egyptian god forms Abraham could have chosen to represent the female of the eternal patriarchal order of celestial marriage, he could not have picked a better example than the goddess Hathor. Father Abraham certainly would have known the history and importance of Hathor from his Egyptian exposure. Egyptian theology teaches that Hathor, like Sarah, was most beautiful and always representative of being "one with their husbands."[108] In Egypt, Hathor could be considered the universal goddess—Mother of all life. This could be compared to the

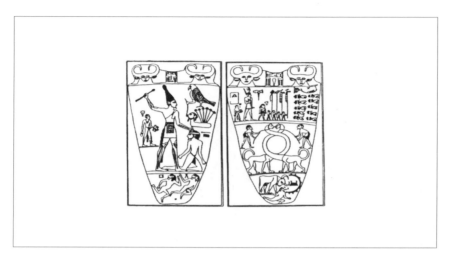

Palette of Narmer

scripture, "And Adam called his wife's name Eve, *because she was the mother of all living*; for thus have I, the Lord God, called the first of all women, which are many."[109]

Hathor's cow image appeared on the Palette of Narmer around 3000 B.C., making her one of the first and oldest of Egyptian goddesses. This first recorded image of her can be seen on both sides of the palette in the top corners as a cow head. (See "Palette of Narmer.") She is credited with being the mother of many gods. This goddess is illustrated in numerous forms. (See "Egyptian Art of the Goddess Hathor.") She wears her identifying headdress of cow's horns and sun disk, with a uracus on her forehead. As the Egyptian sky goddess, who received her bovine name from the cow constellation depicted in the heavens, she is thought to be the first mother of the sun-god. The sun disk held by horns exemplifies the belief that she raised the sun into heaven by her horns. It is interesting that some images show crosses through-out the body intended to represent stars. Her names appear as "chieftainess," "Solar Eye equal to the king," "the golden one," "the queen of the gods," "female soul with two faces," "lady of heaven," "the preserver from the powers of darkness," and

Egyptian art of the goddess Hathor

"goddess of love."[110] Her shrines are some of the most numerous in Egypt, and she was worshiped almost universally. When a child is born, seven images of Hathor are presented to the mother of the child, for the mother has become "the great lady, the beloved of Ra in seven forms."[111] In many kiosks drawings, the wife of the king is represented as the goddess Hathor.[112] The heaven, earth, and underworld were under her realm. She "was more beautiful in her person than any other woman ... for every god was contained in her."[113] She usually is seen with a scepter (rule and reign) in one hand and an anhk (source of eternal life) in the other. Her powers or duties are giving life for eternity, and in the form of a cow she acts as the protector of the king.

This Egyptian goddess symbolized by the cow is one of the few females to have a temple built in her honor. (See "The temple of Hathor.") This is the Ptolemaic temple dedicated to her at Dendera; it is located where the Nile curves after it passes Luxor on the way to the Mediterranean. There is a large vestibule in front of the entrance with colonnades of her image. Hathor's head is carved at the top of the pillars on the facade entrance and inside on the walls of the hypostyle hall. It is interesting that the priests at this temple ascribed to Hathor every spiritual characteristic as the mother

The temple of Hathor

Photo by Peter Clayton

of the gods, the creator of heaven and earth and everything therein. When she is represented as a cow, it is as the Mehweret Cow Goddess of Sky or the Copulating Cow of fertility, being eternally able to beget. *Mehweret* means "great fullness."[114] In many instances of Egyptian art, Hathor is seen as a combination of both human and cow. (See "Cow Images of the goddess Hathor" and "Egyptian art of the goddess Hathor.")

Figure 5 of the earth line shows Hathor in both the female and cow image. The female is standing and holding a giant lotus, symbol of rebirth, over the loins of a great cow, which is usually the commanding or operative figure of the earth line. (See Appendix C, "Hypocephali.") The image of Hathor as a female usually portrays her wearing a sun disk and sometimes with the double plumes emblematic of the power of illumination and enlightenment. The cow motif of Hathor in Figure 5 shows the Menit necklace around the neck, a symbol that personifies the power of nature or a source of living water. The sun disk between the horns is always present, sometimes with the double plumes, which are like the Maat feathers of truth and righteousness. This could be a reminder that it is impossible to seek God successfully without knowledge and purity in our lives. These are the two essential spiritual qualities that father Abraham so diligently sought.

The face of the female image is constructed from a Utchat (Wedjat) Eye, the symbol of healing and perfection. The Utchat Eye represents the perfect eye, the whole one, and is composed by putting six strokes together. Each of the six strokes represent a proportion of the whole eye. The six equate to 1/2, 1/4, 1/8,

Cow images of the goddess Hathor

1/16, 1/32, and 1/64. Together they total sixty-three parts out of sixty-four, being the way Egyptians demonstrate perfection or completion. The 1/64 missing part is considered a bit of magic. (See "Utchat [Wedjat] eye and chart.") According to Egyptology this symbol served as a protection against evil. Having this symbol as her face would indicate that the woman is in possession of all the attributes this emblem signifies. These representations of Figure 5 exemplify perfectly the true significance of the female half of the eternal family unit and are in complete harmony with the ordinances she receives. Joseph said in his explanation that this figure is one of the governing bodies, even the sun, and gets its light from Figure 1 through the grand key (priesthood) or governing power. Does not the sister in the eternal unit get her authority from the priesthood of her husband? Joseph further said it receives its power from Figures 22 and 23, which represent worship and adoration. (See Figures 1, 22, and 23.) This, too, seems in harmony with the mother of life.

Figure 6: Angels of God

Fig. 6—Represents this earth in its four quarters.

The four angels who preside over the four quarters of the earth play an important role in the plan of salvation and the everlasting covenant. The husband and wife of an eternal unit can not automatically claim their children under the patriarchal order of the Melchizedek Priesthood. This must be earned. Once earned, the verification of the sealing of children to parents is pronounced by four representatives of God. The scriptures teach about these four angels in the Book of Revelation. "And I saw another angel ascending from the east, having the seal of the living God: and he cried with a loud voice to the four angels... Hurt not the earth... till we have sealed the servants of our God in their foreheads."[115] On this subject, Joseph Smith said, "We are to understand that they are four angels sent forth from God ... having power to shut up the heavens, to seal up unto life."[116] The Book of Mormon tells us, "And then will I gather them in from the four quarters of the earth; and then will I fulfil the covenant which the Father hath made unto all the people of the house of Israel."[117] It is the four angels that Figure 6 represent that will secure to Latter-day Saint parents, who live the patriarchal order of the Melchizedek Priesthood, their

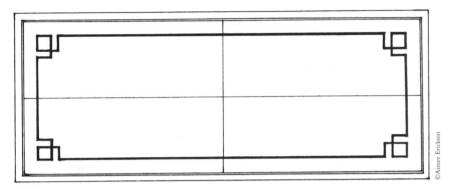

Quadrant design used in LDS construction

posterity, who then become the sons and daughters of God to rule and reign forever. The Lord told Enoch,

> And righteousness and truth will I cause to sweep the earth as with a flood, to gather out mine elect from the four quarters of the earth, unto a place which I shall prepare, an Holy City, that my people may gird up their loins, and be looking forth for the time of my coming; for there shall be my tabernacle, and it shall be called Zion, a New Jerusalem.[118]

This beautiful doctrine concerning four figures can be found in all four standard works.

These four Egyptian figures are used to represent the doctrine that is now understood through modern revelation. It is interesting to know that the four gods and the art of four corners is found in almost of every culture. (See "Quadrant design used in LDS construction" and Appendix E, "Angels of God.") The Egyptians were not far off in their belief that the Pharaoh was a savior from death in the sense that he sealed the ordinances by carrying the four sons of Horus. For further Egyptian concepts of these four motifs, see Facsimile No. 1, Figures 5 through 8. To have the four figures represented on the earth line of this hypocephalus is not only appropriate but significant.

Behind the four figures are the very descriptive symbols of the self-perpetuating biological life cycle. All earth life follows by degrees the biological food chain. These three possibly represent the lion, sheep, and plant (lotus) in the cycle of life, food, and death.

Figure 7: Oracle of God

Fig. 7—Represents God sitting upon his throne, revealing through the heavens the grand Key-words of the Priesthood; as, also, the sign of the Holy Ghost unto Abraham, in the form of a dove.

Joseph's explanation that this figure represents God demonstrates prophetic testimony, as "the seated figure is clearly a form of the Egyptian god Min, the god of the regenerative, procreative forces of nature."[119] Notice that the explanation for this figure is almost verbatim with much of the explanation of Figure 3. Theologically, a male figure of the eternal unit would be the mirror image of God doing His work and helping bring to pass His glory. The powers and representations of this figure illustrate that mortals are God's representatives, holding the keys for priesthood ordinances. The fundamental purpose of priesthood ordinances is to provide the right of passage from one world to the glories of another. Doctrine reveals that God has

> a Holy Priesthood on the earth, and in the heavens, and also in the world of spirits; which Priesthood is after the order or similitude of His Son; and has committed to this Priesthood the keys of holy and divine revelation, and of correspondence, or communication between angels, spirits, and men, and between all the holy departments, principalities, and powers of His government in all worlds.[120]

Joseph in his explanation describes a god revealing and bringing into play every power, the "grand Key-words," of the holy priesthood in behalf of righteous sons and daughters. On another occasion he expounded further, "Knowledge through our Lord and Savior Jesus Christ is the Grand Key that unlocks the glories and the mysteries of Kingdom of Heaven."[121] President David O. McKay told Samoan priesthood holders that this figure "represents God sitting upon his throne, revealing through the heavens the grand Key-Words of the Priesthood." He then commented on the compass and square that is shown.[122] The compass and square symbols, each perfect and complete in itself, when joined together represent a perfect union.

The last part of Joseph's explanation says "also, the sign of the Holy Ghost unto Abraham, in the form of a dove." This seems so appropriate, for revelation comes to mortals through the Holy Ghost, God the Testator, and not much can be done without it. Joseph's declaration that this is God revealing the grand key-words of the priesthood to His representative is testimony that "it shall be given by the comforter, the Holy Ghost, that knoweth all things."[123] These keys collectively are literally the "Keys of the Universe" given to man, those that the Son of Man will receive back from Adam and all dispensation heads at Adam-ondi-Ahman."[124]

In most Egyptian hypocephali the bird in Figure 7 would usually be a snake or an ape. (See Appendix C, "Hypocephali.") It is very significant that a bird is used here, indicative of flight, sky, space, even the heavens from which the source of all priesthood power comes. All Holy Writ, including the writings of Abraham, speak of heavenly messengers bringing down the powers of heaven—and not only for those on earth. It is interesting that *The Last Jubilee: A Sermon (Melchizedek Texts)* of the Dead Sea Scrolls indicates that the power spoken of has efficacy for those on the other side of the veil, in spirit prison, who need liberation as spoken of in Isaiah 61:1. "The Lord has sent me to proclaim liberation to the captives." And in the Hebrew language the word "liberation is harmonious with 'swallow'—which is, of course, a celestial creature signifying that they will become one with the sons of heaven."[125] That which is brought is for those in mortality and for the spirits on the other side of the veil. The bird in Figure 3 is also presenting a Utchat (Wedjat) Eye, the symbol of glory, light, and healing, even perfection,[126] or completion,[127] to an enthroned male Amon. (See "Utchat [Wedjat] eye and chart" and Figure 3 of this facsimile.) The presentation of the Utchat Eye would indicate that the representative does not possess it. In order to obtain the attributes represented by this eye, he must make himself clean from the world through the priesthood by doing the work of God.[128] During Christian times this mystical eye was the symbol the Coptics used for "salvation."

The upraised arm and the flail of Figure 7 depict regenerative powers. Both Figures 5 and 7, the male and female, are presented as having powers of regeneration. The commandment to all couples destined for the highest glory of the celestial kingdom is to multiply and replenish the earth. It is the same decree that was first given to father Adam and mother Eve. These divine generative powers conjoined with the blessings of the priesthood are the source of eternal posterity and the fulfillment of the this great commandment.

Both the Egyptian art and Joseph's explanation of Figure 7 indicate that it is representative of man, a potential god of heaven, receiving all the priesthood powers for his eternal family on both sides of the veil. Hanna declared that her son Samuel received his authority this same way. She said, concerning the Lord giving power to her son, that "out of heaven shall he thunder … and he shall give strength unto his king, and exalt the horn of his anointed." Another testament of the male half of the eternal unit comes from the dialogue between the Lord and Noah. Noah asked why the flood? The Lord answered specifically, "For behold mine anger is kindled against the sons of men for they will not hearken to my voice [refusing to honor their priesthood powers]."[129] The Egyptian symbolism of Figure 7 correctly represents all of the above gospel principles.

Figure 8: Temple Knowledge

Fig. 8—Contains writings that cannot be revealed unto the world; but is to be had in the Holy Temple of God.

It is within these figures that the identity of the owner of this hypocephalus is given. Sheshonk, or Shashanq, to whom this hypocephalus is ascribed to, and the name Osiris are the two hieroglyphic words readily identified and unanimously agreed upon by Egyptologists. Sheshonk was the founder of the Twenty-second Dynasty, from which a cryptogramatic inscription has been found in which the king boasts that he is Osiris, "the Great One who grants

life as the Living One."[130] This comes from a statement in the Book
of Breathings, harking back to the Book of the Dead, indicating that
the person receiving the initiation ordinances is given the name of
Osiris. The Pharaoh's name in Figure 8 is included with the name
of Osiris because it indicates that the authority of the ordinances
comes to the Pharaoh from Osiris. The other three symbols, from
right to left, are again the hieroglyphic ideograms for "durability-
backbone" (Djed-column), "life" (ankh), and "power" (Was, war
scepter). Remember, these same three ideograms can be seen in
the symbolic scepter held as an indication of power in Figure 1.
Together they represent all life, all endurance, and all power which
would enable the candidate to pass from this world to the next.
(See "Ankh, Djed-column, and Was scepter.") To summarize the
five hieroglyphic ideograms then, the first is the name of the Egyptian Pharaoh Shashanq who represents the embodiment of the god
Osiris, who possessed all power, life, and durability. "The explanation
given about Fig. 8 should convince the thoughtful Latter-day Saint
that Abraham was acquainted with the sacred endowments and hence
a temple or its equivalent in which they could be administered."[131]

Figures 9–11: Sacred Knowledge

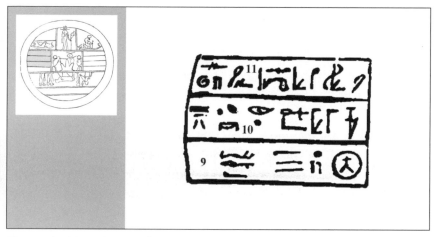

Figures 9, 10, and 11 ought not to be revealed at the present time.

One must understand that "the secret things belong unto the Lord our God: but those things which are revealed [or will be revealed] belong unto us and to our children for ever, that we may do all the words of this law."[132]

Figures 12–15

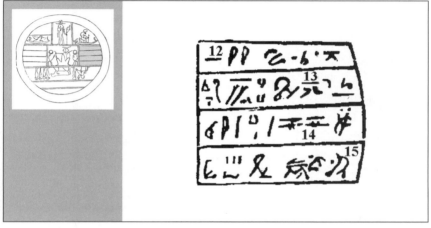

Figures 12, 13, 14, 15, 16, 17, 18, 19, 20, and 21 will be given in the own due time of the Lord.

Figures 16–17

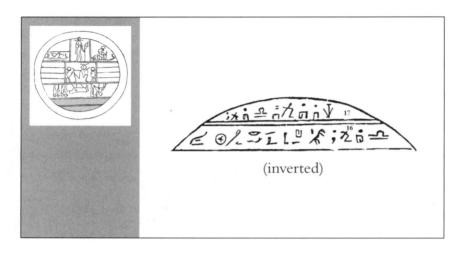

(inverted)

Figures 19–21

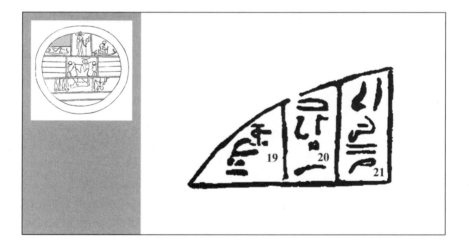

"The Lord has ordained that all the most holy things...all the most holy conversations and correspondence with God, angels, and spirits, shall be had only in the sanctuary of His holy temple on the earth, when prepared for that purpose by His Saints."[133]

Figure 18: Circle of Prayer

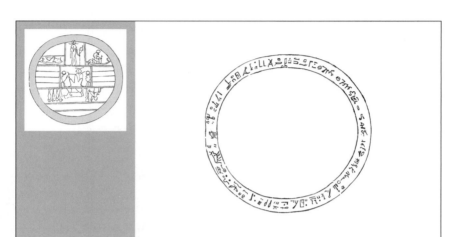

Although Joseph said this "will be given in the own due time of the Lord," it has been plainly demonstrated that this part of the facsimile is a circle of prayer. The writing around the outer edge is a request for divine guidance. This is clearly evoked in the rim inscriptions of most hypocephali, which begin either with the prayer or the answer to the prayer: "Oh Dbbty" (one in passage between heaven and earth); "O Most Hidden one o akh," or the answer, "I am an Akh (w) coming down" or "I am Dbbty or most Hidden one—I am he that opens, I am he that closes." "Iwnw or Heliopolis" is recorded twice within this circle and can definitely be associated with the Heleopolitan cult. Heliopolis, the sun city, the On of the Old Testament, was "the most important cult-center of Egypt."[134] This rim enclosure is sometimes called the "Eye of Iris" or "Water of Nun."

A circle of prayer illustrates a complete, perfect 360 degrees. This would support the premise that all power in heaven and earth is represented within a true circle of prayer. This circle of prayer always depicts an ascension story similar to those of father Adam and down through the Old and New Testaments. Abraham himself verified that it was from such a circle in heaven that God chose those who would be the rulers of his creation.[135] Certainly Abraham knew from the Egyptians that the writing around the rim contained words of prayer or supplication. This example of an ascension pattern could not have been more in harmony with our own dispensation of the fullness of times, which began with the prayer offered by Joseph Smith Jr. in the sacred grove, followed by revelatory supplication throughout his entire life. Are we committed to personal supplication for our own source of revelatory knowledge?

Scriptures also equate to the mysteries and a circle.

> For he that diligently seeketh shall find; and the mysteries of God shall be unfolded unto them, by the power of the Holy Ghost, as well in these times as in times of old, and as well in times of old as in times to come; wherefore, the course of the Lord is one eternal round.[136]

Members of the Church have been told concerning our temples:

> Ye Latter-day Saints! Ye thousands of the hosts of Israel! Ye are assembled here today, and have laid these Corner Stones, for the express purpose that the living might hear from the dead, and that we may prepare a holy sanctuary, where 'the people may seek unto their God, and for the living to hear from the dead,' and that heaven and earth, and the world of spirits may commune together—that the kings, nobles, presidents, rulers, judges, priests, counselors, and senators, which compose the general assembly of the Church of the First-Born in all these different spheres of temporal and spiritual existence, may sit in grand council and hold a congress or court on the earth, [and] so concert measures for the overthrow of the 'mystery of iniquity,' the thrones of tyrants, the sanctuaries of priestcraft and superstition, and the reign of ignorance, sin, and death.[137]

Figures 22–23: Male and Female

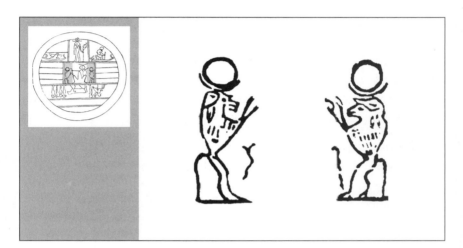

Joseph states in his explanation of Facsimile No. 2 that these are "the stars represented by numbers 22 and 23, receiving light from the revolutions of Kolob." Here are a male and female baboon (apes with dog heads) in an attitude of honor and adoration to their God. This idea is substantiated by the Proclamation on the Family, which states,

> In the premortal realm spirit sons and daughters knew and worshiped God as their Eternal Father and accepted His plan by which His children could obtain a physical body and gain earthly experience to progress toward perfection and ultimately realize his or her divine destiny as an heir to eternal life.[138]

It is also significant in this drawing that the male is on the right and the female on the left, indicating the polarity of world customs. In Egypt "right and left were also applied to the sexes as expressions of the polarity of world order; for men the right side was regarded as good and for women the left."[139] The king was equated with the right eye and the sun, while the queen was equated with the left eye and the moon. These figures are adorned with either sun-moon crowns or horns-sun disks resting on their heads Either headpiece would have significance. The sun-moon crowns could symbolize their potential for eternal powers connected to horn and sun disk, or white stone, or the eternal responsibilities of the sun and the moon. In Egyptian hieroglyphics apes are often used in connection with stars and constellations. The scriptures interchange stars with seed in describing Abraham's blessings of posterity.

In front of each of these figures is a serpent symbolizing adversity, lies, corruption, and anything that will stop spiritual progression.

> The devil came to save the world and stood up as a savior. The contention in heaven was that Jesus contended that there would be certain souls that would be condemned and not saved, but the devil said, 'I am a savior,' and that he could save them all. As the grand council gave in for Jesus Christ, the lot fell on him. So the devil rose up, rebelled against God, fell and was thrust down, with all who put up their heads for him.[140]

The forces of opposition are with us, and all mortals must pass by the serpents of the world to be reborn and give honor, glory, and majesty to God.

Summary

From the art of Facsimile No. 2 and the explanations of Joseph Smith, we know that the top half of this facsimile represents heaven and illustrates four motifs of heavenly authority. Figure 1 shows a male and female image with the Egyptian symbols for authority of the "holy order and the ordinances thereof"[141] within a celestial framework. Figure 2, a male and female image, illustrates the first grand governing creation holding the key of power as revealed from the first government of which it is a mirror image. At the feet is the lotus-altar signature symbol of Abraham. Figure 3 is a motif representing a God of power and authority, the source of light, with the holy keys of the priesthood as revealed to father

Adam and all subsequent fathers. Figure 4 shows a bird equal in authority to the other images through the expanse or firmament of heaven and in measurement of time. The top half of Facsimile No. 2 is almost a pictorial of the prophet Joseph Smith's first vision and last two discourses, the first being the vision he received in the sacred grove where three deities revealed eternal truths,[142] the last being the two great sermons about the Godhead just before his death, much of which he said he learned from Abraham.[143] The bottom half shows a woman and a cow, representative of female royalty with the powers of procreation, one who obtains her light and power from the priesthood and is perpetuated through her seed. The four angels with sealing powers for the four quarters of the earth are also represented. Figure 7 depicts a representative of God receiving the grand key-words of the priesthood. These figures are the recipients of all the powers of heaven. The bottom half of the facsimile is almost a pictorial for the profound "The Family: A Proclamation to the World."

Many other aspects of Father in heaven's plan of salvation, redemption, and happiness as it relates to the temple are illustrated, the greatest being that the temple is truly a great conduit between heaven and earth in which a complete understanding of the everlasting covenant can be obtained. The entire hypocephalus is a pictorial of a circle of prayer where powers and blessings from heaven are given to righteous recipients on earth fulfilling the covenant made between members of the Godhead.

Chapter 7:
Facsimile No. 3

he original of Facsimile No. 3 came from the Scroll of Hor, which was given to the Chicago Wood Museum in 1864 and destroyed in the Chicago Fire of 1871.[1] The scene it represents (See Facsimile No. 3 on following page) should have great significance for every member of the Church. One can see that which is illustrated in Facsimile No. 3

> enable(s) them to pass by the angels and the gods, until they get into the presence of the Father, represented by Abraham His authorized representative. They are made kings and priests, queens and priestesses to God, to rule and reign as such over their posterity and those who may be given to them by adoption, in the great jubilee of rest ... spoken of by John the revelator. This great coronation is bestowed on the elect according to the foreknowledge of God the Father, through sanctification of the Spirit, unto obedience ... of the blood of Jesus Christ.[2]

This coronation is only pronounced upon an eternal unit of husband and wife who have become one through the new and everlasting covenant. Joseph Smith's explanation that this is a portrayal of "Abraham sitting upon Pharaoh's throne" identifies

Facsimile No. 3

Explanation (as given in the *Pearl of Great Price*):

Fig. 1   Abraham sitting upon Pharaoh's throne, by the politeness of the king, with a crown upon his head, representing the Priesthood, as emblematical of the grand Presidency in Heaven; with the scepter of justice and judgment in his hand.

Fig. 2   King Pharaoh, whose name is given in the characters above his head.

Fig. 3   Signifies Abraham in Egypt as given also in Figure 10 of Facsimile No. 1.

Fig. 4   Prince of Pharaoh, King of Egypt, as written above the hand.

Fig. 5   Shulem, one of the king's principal waiters, as represented by the characters above his hand.

Fig. 6   Olimlah, a slave belonging to the prince.

Abraham is reasoning upon the principles of Astronomy, in the king's court.

Coronation and kiosk scenes

this facsimile as a ritual coronation scene. Coronation and kiosk scenes are found in almost every Egyptian temple and represent a large variety of ritual events, judgments, offerings, and titles, or a combination of all four. (See "Coronation and kiosk scenes.") These Egyptian scenes are "a symbolic repetition of the coronation for it is in the temple that the coronation takes place ... the royal party moving from chamber to chamber during the rites."[3]

Facsimile No. 3 depicts a king, prince, queen, commoner, servant, and slave, all parts of normal court life. With this background, Abraham has given us a beautiful coronation scene that should illustrate one's desire for the fullness of the blessings of the Father as stated in the scripture, "O Lord God Almighty, hear us in these our petitions, and answer us from heaven, Thy holy habitation, where Thou sittest enthroned, with glory, honor, power, majesty, might, dominion, truth, justice, judgment, mercy, and an infinity of fullness, from everlasting to everlasting."[4] Brother Nibley verified that the motif of this facsimile shows the coronation of the two equal capacities into godhood royalty. The type of coronation presented here could represent any coronation, but a coronation having to do with the everlasting covenant, and especially the fullness of the priesthood of God, would involve a king and queen.

The procurement and understanding of these mysteries of God is the greatest of all blessings given to individuals in any dispensation. Members of the Church know that when they are sealed by God's representatives, then "they are they who are priests and kings [and priestesses and queens], who have received of his fulness, and of his glory."[5] It is with these blessings that an eternal unit reaches the full measure of its creation. This is verified by modern-day scriptures, which inform us that "Abraham received all things ... and hath entered into his exaltation and sitteth upon his throne."[6] The great message of this facsimile is that all righteous covenant recipients, through the everlasting covenant, may receive this coronation and "sit down in the kingdom of God, with Abraham and Sarah."[7] Faithful members are told, "This promise is yours also, because ye are of Abraham, and the promise was made unto Abraham; and by this law is the continuation of the works of my Father, wherein he glorifieth himself."[8]

Abraham and Sarah have received their coronation, just as every worthy couple who have been sealed can receive their coronation by obedience to the everlasting covenants. We know Abraham and Sarah proved their faithfulness and received covenant blessings unconditionally when they were given the fullness of the priesthood while in mortality.[9] Bruce R. McConkie said,

> When a man lives the law that qualifies him for eternal life, the Lord is bound by his own law to confer that greatest of all gifts upon him. The calling, which up to that time was provisional, is then made sure. The receipt of the promised blessings are no longer conditional; they are guaranteed. Announcement is made that every gospel blessing shall be inherited.[10]

The highest type of priesthood coronation is receiving in mortality what Joseph Smith referred to as being "called, elected and made sure,"[11] the fulfillment of one's foreordination in the spirit world.

The differences from the Egyptian norm in this facsimile are fascinating and very revealing. First, there is no veil in this kiosk. All requirements have been met. The candidates have a right to be in the presence of God's representative. Abraham again used his "Abraham in Egypt" signature (Figure 3) and identified himself as sitting on the throne representing supreme authority. Joseph Smith also gives this figure the ultimate authority by using the title "King Pharaoh." Hathor-Isis (Figure 2), goddess of fertility and mother of life, would be a beautiful representation of Sarah or "Mother in heaven."[12] Together, these two represent the priesthood and the creative powers of Deity. The male and female figures shown here have different faces and crowns than found in Egyptian art. Each figure has a different eye, perhaps suggesting that all eyes are to be "single to the glory of God." The slave is especially unique. We now have Abraham with Sarah, represented by Hathor-Isis, as servants of Deity, giving the right of passage to the two candidates for eternal life with the servant (slave) of the Lord presenting them.

The scene depicted in this facsimile is very special; it even takes place in a crowning room. Certainly with both five and six pointed stars at the top of the scene it may be called a star room because of their great symbolic significance. The stars are unique here; they are not found in any other Egyptian kiosks or coronation scenes. The veil, hawk, and four sealing angels which are always found in Egyptian kiosks are missing. This too is very revealing, for they are not needed at the coronation, as the fruits of their labors have already justified the candidates. The veil has parted. The hawk and angels have accomplished their work, making the candidates worthy of coronation.

Joseph Smith's explanation about this facsimile is also very revealing. Although there is hieratic writing in Facsimiles 1 and 2, it is only in Facsimile 3 that Joseph draws attention to the names written above Figures 2, 4, and 5. Father Abraham would have understood the importance of names, as the Lord changed his and Sarah's names.

This facsimile also has wavy lines, instead of the straight lines normally found in an Egyptian throne drawing, as the foundation of the throne which Abraham is sitting on. The changing from straight lines to wavy lines is representative of water. Could this be symbolic of living water? Certainly a prophet representing God would be a source of the Savior's living water. One can also see changes from Egyptian norm in each figure's face and in their style of clothing. Even the robes are drawn differently from typical Egyptian robes, including some kind of apron on Figures 1, 5, and 6. The candidates (Figures 4 and 5) are holding hands with the other hand raised. Is this indicative of their oneness and testifying that they are standing clean and pure, worthy of oneness with Deity, even as the Gods are one within the everlasting covenant? The Lord certainly indicated the necessity of this in His great intercessory prayer.[13] With a coronation comes the assurance of the Savior of their oneness and that they "shall be loved of my Father, and I will love him [the candidates], and will manifest myself to him [the candidates]." The presence of the Lord, the second comforter, is the crowning blessing of the everlasting covenant.[14]

Abraham depicted this coronation scene, Joseph Smith described it dually, and God has verified that Abraham and Sarah have received their coronation and have reached a fullness, the measure of their creation.[15] Members of the Church know that "an intelligent being, in the image of God possesses every organ, attribute, sense, sympathy, affection that is possessed by God Himself"[16] and that every worthy individual can obtain the blessings of godhood: "For I am the Lord thy God, and will be with thee even unto the end of the world; and through all eternity: for verily I seal upon you your exaltation, and prepare a throne for you in the kingdom of my Father, with Abraham your father."[17] These blessings of the fullness are beautifully described by John the Beloved.

> And one of the elders answered, saying unto me, What are these which are arrayed in white robes? and whence came they? And I said unto him, Sir, thou knowest. And he said to me, These are they which came out of great tribulation, and have washed their robes, and made them white in the blood of the Lamb. Therefore are they before the throne of God, and serve him day and night in his temple: and he that sitteth on the throne shall dwell among them.[18]

This is again verified in modern scripture:

> Then shall they be gods, because they have no end; therefore shall they be from everlasting to everlasting, because they continue; then shall they be above all, because all things are subject unto them. Then shall they be gods, because they have all power, and the angels are subject unto them.[19]

Scripture also tells us that Abraham

> abode in my law; as Isaac also and Jacob did none other things than that which they were commanded; and because they did none other things than that which they were commanded, they have entered into their exaltation, according to the promises, and sit upon thrones, and are not angels but are gods.[20]

Peter is specific on the necessity of obtaining this coronation. "Wherefore the rather, brethren, give diligence to make your calling and election sure: for if ye do these things, ye shall never fall: For so an entrance shall be ministered unto you abundantly into the everlasting kingdom of our Lord and Savior Jesus Christ."[21] Very early in Church history, in 1834, before he received the Book of

Abraham, the Prophet Joseph asked two questions. "Have you a promise of receiving a crown of righteousness from the hand of the Lord, with the Church of the Firstborn?" and "If the Saints are not to reign, for what purpose are they crowned?"[22] It is interesting that Joseph Smith gave instructions for obtaining the fullness of the priesthood the very first time he gave the endowments in this dispensation. He spoke of "washings, anointings, endowments ...to secure the fulness of those blessings which have been prepared for the Church of the Firstborn, and come up and abide in the presence of Elohim in the eternal worlds."[23] This was verified by Joseph Fielding Smith, President of the Church, in his first address to the priesthood on 4 April 1970.

> You cannot receive the fullness of the priesthood and the fullness of eternal reward unless you receive the ordinances of the house of the Lord: ... the door is then open so you can obtain all the blessings which any man can gain. There is no exaltation in the kingdom of God without the fullness of the priesthood, and every man who receives the Melchizedek Priesthood does so with an oath and covenant that he shall be exalted.[24]

Other modern prophets have also admonished members to go forth and seek the fullness of the priesthood.[25] The final verse of the Book of Mormon may itself be an illustration of this principle, as it describes the coronation of Moroni himself as we meet at "the pleasing bar of the great Jehovah."[26]

In his closing chapter of the Book of Mormon, in fact, Moroni gives specific instructions about obtaining the highest coronation of the everlasting covenant. First, the "daughters of Zion" are to put on the beautiful garments, to become "perfect." Then he mentions the process for the sons who, with their priesthood, are to "become holy without spot" by coming "unto Christ." Charles W. Penrose enlarged upon this beautiful concept of daughters and sons: "When a woman is sealed to a man holding the Priesthood, she becomes one with him ...The glory and power and dominion that he will exercise when he has the fulness of the Priesthood and becomes a 'king and a priest unto God,' she will share with him."[27]

Egyptian star artwork

Moving to Joseph's explanation of this facsimile for a moment, we note that he described the scene by saying, "Abraham is reasoning upon the principles of astronomy, in the king's court." We have in this facsimile the five-pointed stars and a few six-pointed stars (lining the top of the kiosk). Both have great significance. It is also significant that Hathor in Figure 2 is holding a six-sided star in place of an ankh. To the ancient Egyptians, the five-pointed star was associated with the resurrection, temple vestments, the office of

Star man

seer, and the office of king and priest. The scriptures suggest that this star represents a pre-existent spirit, a ruler or governor in the Lord's kingdom,[28] or a glorified resurrected being. This five-sided star also stands for Christ when pointed up and Solomon when pointed down. It is commonly called the Star of Israel. (See "Egyptian star artwork.") Man himself is represented in the five-sided star found in this star-covered sacred room. He has five senses, five extremities, five fingers, five toes, and his body is composed of five elements. When he stands erect with feet and hands extended, he resembles a five-sided star, with the head being the fifth extension, pointing upward. (See "Star man.")

In our dispensation we have been told,

> Abraham received promises concerning his seed, and of the fruit of his loins—from whose loins ye are, namely, my servant Joseph—which were to continue so long as they were in the world; and as touching Abraham and his seed, out of the world

they should continue; both in the world and out of the world should they continue as innumerable as the stars.[29]

Certainly the culmination of all things is the "eternal family." One only has to read "The Family: A Proclamation to the World" by the First Presidency and Council of the Twelve Apostles of The Church of Jesus Christ of Latter-day Saints to understand what family and seed are all about. This proclamation is timely and profound. All the organizations within the Church and all the ordinances within the temple are specifically designed to aid mothers and fathers in becoming a successful family unit in the kingdom of God.

In the final analysis, everything in Facsimile No. 3 seems to be a ritual dramatization utilizing the "principal of acquisition, or endowment of power by impersonation. The man who sits on the throne is identical with his predecessor and his successor—not symbolically but actually."[30]

> To the increase of his (Jesus's) kingdom there shall be no end. That promise is also made to us—to the increase of our kingdom there shall be no end ... There was to be no end to the kingdom of Abraham, he was to have thrones, principalities and dominions; to be crowned not with a barren, empty crown, not a crown without a kingdom, but a real one, emblematical of endless and boundless rule, power, dominion and glory. The Lord has promised the same glory to every being who attains to the glory of the sun, who gains a fullness of glory in the celestial kingdom. They all will be heirs of God and joint heirs with Jesus Christ.[31]

Joseph quoted John the Revelator, saying, "To him that overcometh will I grant to sit with me in my throne, even as I also overcame, and am set down with my Father in his throne."[32] This is the completion of the second goal of the Church, the crown of perfection.[33] For a Saint to be perfected by receiving and completing all that the Godhead has given them through the everlasting covenant, being sealed up to eternal life, to be made kings and priests, queens and priestesses, would be called a coronation of eternal glory. They shall wear crowns and sit upon their thrones. This coronation bestows powers and blessings which are immediately available and can be enjoyed in mortality as well as through the eternities to come. Once the ordinance of eternal marriage attains the efficacy brought about by coronation, a far different state of responsibilities and obligations are put in place for the faithful couple.[34] "They become the sons of Moses and of Aaron and the seed of Abraham, and the church and kingdom, and the elect of God."[35] There is no reason to marvel "that the Lord requires sacred places for such great and glorious things—'the fullness of the holy priesthood' to be restored.' "[36]

The coronation of king and queen, priest and priestess, prophet and prophetess provides a unique endowment of communications with heaven.[37] There is a mighty change of heart that brings about a virtuous countenance, while the recipient abhors sin and engages in doing good continually. In this process these souls seek for an increase in spiritual training by daily spiritual communion. Their bodies can then be overruled and their spirits truly assume control, completing the process of changing from the natural man to a spiritual disciple. They become comfortable in the presence of the Lord and with members of the Church of the Firstborn, for the Father now has given into their hands all things.[38] They are privileged to hear "the voice of his excellent glory"[39] and receive a guarantee that one will receive the things to which one has been ordained. They are given power and authority to unlock the sacred treasures of eternity and become acquainted with hidden stores of knowledge, while deep mysteries are made plain.[40]

And as was pronounced upon Abraham and Sarah,

> then shall they be gods, because they have no end; therefore shall they be from everlasting to everlasting, because they continue; then shall they be above all, because all things are subject unto them. Then shall they be gods, because they have all power, and the angels are subject unto them.[41]

It seems appropriate to again quote from the Doctrine and Covenants:

> then shall thy confidence wax strong in the presence of God; and the doctrine of the priesthood shall distil upon thy soul as the dews from heaven. The Holy Ghost shall be thy constant companion, and thy scepter an unchanging scepter of righteousness and truth; and thy dominion shall be an everlasting dominion, and without compulsory means it shall flow unto thee forever and ever.[42]

With this coronation, the posterity of these eternal units will multiply in ever-increasing numbers to fill worlds in the next eternity.[43] This facsimile truly seems to be representative of the fullness of the priesthood, the everlasting covenant, and the work and glory of God.

Figure 1: God's Representative

Fig. 1—Abraham sitting upon Pharaoh's throne, by the politeness of the king, with a crown upon his head, representing the Priesthood, as emblematical of the grand Presidency in Heaven; with the scepter of justice and judgment in his hand.

Parenthetically, Joseph Smith could have said this figure is also Abraham, the patriarch-prophet, sitting upon God's throne by the politeness of Jehovah, with a crown upon his head, representing God's priesthood with the scepter of light, glory, power, and dominion.[44] This explanation makes the facsimile emblematic of the powers of heaven, that of Father, Son, and Holy Ghost, the implementers of the "everlasting covenant." Brother Nibley said the scepter here is "a true heralds's staff, in intent a king's scepter, held by the herald as a deputy as a sign to the world that God has given his authority to the holder ... since it represents the power of the priesthood ... a simple symbolic representation."[45] The word *scepter* originally meant a rod or a shaft. The word is used metaphorically in the scriptures to identify supreme power.[46] In this figure, the candidate is receiving the fullness from the hand of one who holds God's divine authority.

Figure 1 is wearing the Atef-crown, the oldest and holiest of Pharaoh's many crowns. The white crown, dating back to Narmer in 3350 B.C. as seen on the famous Tablet of Narmer, was one of the first crowns ever used in Egypt. The plumes—two large, curved feathers—were added later, symbolizing the two sources of life and light, or spirit and truth. These feathers are similar to the Maat feather, the symbol of righteousness, on the head of Figure 4. The two crowns illustrated in this facsimile with the two plumes, along with the crown of Hathor, seem very significant. (See "White crown and Maat feathers.") All together, this could be a perfect representation of the highest form of coronation powers. The crown shown here is symbolic of the position and status that kings, queens, priests, and priestesses will hold in eternity. They will be crowned with light, glory, power, and dominion. As such, this figure would have all rights to authorize and perform a coronation to worthy recipients.

The Lord said, "To him that overcometh will I grant to sit with me in my throne, even as I also overcame, and am set down with my Father in his throne."[47] Joseph Smith raised two interesting questions, referring to "crowns": "Have you a promise of receiving

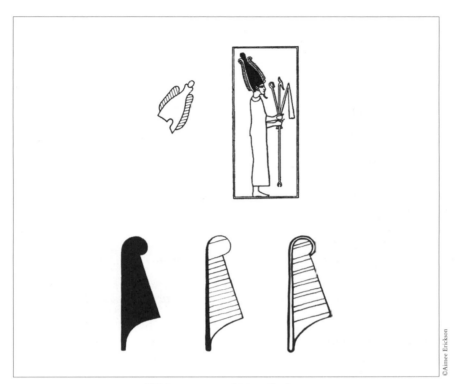

White crown and Maat feathers

a crown of righteousness [signified here by the Maat feathers] from the hand of the Lord, with the Church of the Firstborn?" And, "If the Saints are not to reign, for what purpose are they crowned?"[48] This power to reign is inherent in the Melchizedek Priesthood:

> The power and authority of the higher, or Melchizedek Priesthood, is to hold the keys of all the spiritual blessings of the Church—To have the privilege of receiving the mysteries of the kingdom of heaven, to have the heavens opened unto them, to commune with the general assembly and Church of the Firstborn, and to enjoy the communion and presence of God the Father, and Jesus the Mediator of the new covenant.[49]

Because this figure is in possession of or is an authorized representative of this power and authority, the coronation illustrated in Facsimile No. 3 can take place and be accepted by the Father.

Figure 2: Female Royalty

Fig. 2—King Pharaoh, whose name is given in the characters above his head.

Joseph's statement about Figure 2, "King Pharaoh, whose name is given in the characters above his head" is baffling, as the figure portrayed is that of a woman. The confusion dissipates with the realization that this drawing is Hathor-Isis,[50] the great goddess consort of the gods. (See "Egyptian art of the goddess Hathor" in Chapter 6.) Remember Brother Nibley spoke of her as "Hathor the Great, the Lady of Heaven, the Queen of the Gods and Goddesses."[51] Is this not the perfect example of the creative stewardship of Deity to multiply and replenish—and in addition a beautiful representation for this half of responsibility of an eternal unit. Notice a Wedjat Eye representing her face. This figure in its entirety could be representative of the eternal wife, mother of life, clean every whit, the origin of all stars, and creator of "eternal lives." (See Facsimile 2, Fig. 5, in Chapter 6.)

It is also significant that she is holding a star in her hand. This star is a six-pointed star, which has replaced the common ankh symbol typically seen in Egyptian coronation or kiosk scenes. (See "Coronation and kiosk scenes.") This simplest of modifications propels us

CHRIST   DAVID   SOLOMON

©Aimee Erickson

Five- and six-pointed stars

from the Egyptian symbol of life to a symbol of God, perfection, and posterity. A six-pointed, twelve-sided star is made from two equilateral triangles that are overlaid, symbolic of husband and wife, two equal genders brought into one unit of perfection. The six-pointed star is also a symbol of the Godhead and is commonly called the "Star of David." (See "Five- and six-pointed stars.")

Figure 3: Abraham in Egypt

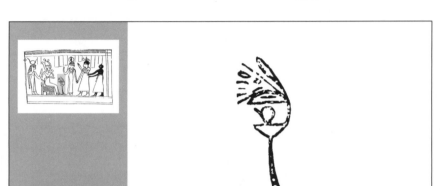

Fig. 3—Signifies Abraham in Egypt as given also in Figure 10 of Facsimile No. 1.

Joseph reveals that this figure "signifies Abraham in Egypt," as he did in Figure 10 of Facsimile No. 1. (It is also found in Figure 2 of Facsimile 2.) Brother Nibley said, "The lotus, perhaps the richest of all Egyptian symbols, can stand for the purest abstraction…it points to two things. In Facsimile 3 we are told that "it points to…a man and a country,"[52] and before the altar, before the throne, signifies, "that this takes place in Egypt."[53] One can see that this image is a lotus and altar-offering table but differs slightly from those shown in the other facsimiles.

Figure 4: Daughter of God

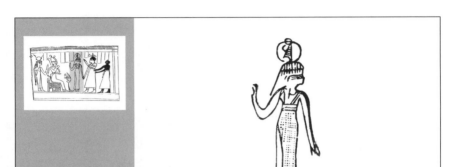

Fig. 4—Prince of Pharaoh, King of Egypt, as written above the hand.

Joseph describes Figure 4 as "Prince of Pharaoh, King of Egypt, as written above the hand." To represent king Pharaoh in Figure 2, Abraham used Hathor as the Goddess Mother, and in Figure 4, for the "Prince of Pharaoh," he uses another female, the Lady Maat,[54] identified by the Maat feather within a circle above the head. The circle is called a cartouche, which is drawn around the name of every Pharaoh; it signifies that the king is ruler of all "that which is encircled by the sun."[55] In representing males as females Abraham has used two of the most important Egyptian goddesses of eternal Egyptian longevity. Using the Lady Maat as the candidate for coronation seems appropriate, as she represents the very embodiment of legitimate rule and a female candidate for the fullness of the priesthood. This candidate clutches the Breathing Document (knowledge) as her passport. These two ladies should be present in any coronation scene when there is a transmission of royal power. For Joseph Smith to say in his explanation "King Pharaoh" and "Prince of Pharaoh" when the figures were those of females is another testimony of his prophetic calling.

Figure 5: Son of God

Fig. 5—Shulem, one of the king's principal waiters, as represented by the characters above his hand.

Joseph identifies this figure as "Shulem, one of the king's principal waiters, as identified by the characters above his hand." The "king's principal waiters" would be the proven souls that the Lord would make his rulers.[56] In a coronation, this figure would represent the male prophet-patriarch of the eternal unit. He holds the hand of his eternal companion and wears the same footwear as she does, but he wears the same robes as the slave (servant). The crown on his head is indicative of his being "clean every whit" and is a counterpart to the Maat feather on Figure 4 and the Wedjat Eye within Figure 2. All represent worthiness to have the fullness of the priesthood which father Abraham desired.[57]

Figure 6: Servant of God

Fig. 6—Olimlah, a slave belonging to the prince.

Joseph Smith's explanation says this figure is "Olimlah, a slave belonging to the prince." The title of "slave" as used today certainly does not seem indicative of a coronation ritual, the results of which are kingdoms, authority, powers, even complete freedom and peace.

In tracing the movement of the mummies during and after the Prophet's exposure to them, it was found that one Dr. J. R. Riggs wrote down his opinion of the mummies after he examined them and while they were all still together. He designated them as being "a King, a Queen, a Princess, and a slave."[58]

However, the term *slave* refers to a person who is the property of and wholly subject to another. In the gospel is this not what a servant of Deity is? Does God not own us? Are we not subject to the Godhead? "Therefore is the kingdom of heaven likened unto a certain king, which would take account of his servants."[59] Also, there are always authorized representatives who attend the candidates during a coronation. This segment of the scene is explained perfectly in the Doctrine and Covenants. "For he that receiveth my servants receiveth me; And he that receiveth me receiveth my

Father; And he that receiveth my Father receiveth my Father's kingdom; therefore all that my Father hath shall be given unto him."[60] Servants can certainly touch the candidates as they administer to them, and, as authorized representatives of Deity, they can present a person to the Father. The scriptures are full of accounts of such servants.[61]

A coronation into the realm of Deity gives a man and woman a legal right to draw upon all truth, power, and blessings of the Godhead. It then becomes the responsibility of this priest and king, priestess and queen, an eternal unit of the divine patriarchal order, to devote their lives to building up the kingdom of God and establishing Zion. Dr. Hyrum Andrus summarized this facsimile in his book *Principles of Perfection* with this statement:

> Joseph Smith taught that celestial society is patriarchal in its structure, and that all who are born into the kingdom of God must be organized by the covenants and powers of the priesthood into a divine patriarchal order under Christ, who is their Father in the living attributes and powers of eternal life.[62]

Chapter 8:
Conclusion

I t has often been said that the past can explain the present and give light to the future. Church history shows just how important these drawings from Abraham's papyri, created long in the past, were to Joseph's understanding of the mysteries of the kingdom, even the mysteries of godliness. Church history confirms that the papyrus scrolls were obtained in July 1835 and that the "priesthood keys" for temple work were restored in April 1836. However, knowledge of the contents of the Book of Abraham and the facsimiles did not come to the Prophet until he translated them during the last part of 1840 and early 1841, when he finally had some peace and security in Nauvoo. The book and facsimiles were then published in 1842, just two months before Joseph gave the endowment for the first time. The facsimiles, as Joseph's explanations of them confirm, brought to him an understanding of the sacred ordinances of temple work and seem, historically, to be the final thread Joseph needed for weaving the temple tapestry. Once Joseph had the work of father Abraham, temple work could start. The endowment was first given in May 1842. The following year, 1843, brought the recording of section 132 of the Doctrine and Covenants, followed by the long-awaited sealing ceremony for faithful couples within the everlasting covenant.

Looked at sequentially, father Abraham's facsimiles provide a "vision" of what is available and necessary for both salvation and exaltation. Enoch saw and understood the vision of the plan of salvation and recorded a great outline of it.

> Therefore it is given to abide in you ... the peaceable things of immortal glory; the truth of all things; that which quickeneth all things, which maketh alive all things; that which knoweth all things, and hath all power according to wisdom, mercy, truth, justice, and judgment. And now, behold, I say unto you: This is the plan of salvation unto all men, through the blood of mine Only Begotten, who shall come in the meridian of time.[1]

Enoch could very well be speaking of the facsimiles of Abraham, for he speaks of glory, truth, eternal life, knowledge, and power, all of which are exemplified through the Egyptian symbolism of the facsimiles. As did ancient prophets of God, President John Taylor, speaking of the "Eternal Vista," captured these same truths as illustrated in the facsimiles. He said,

> Standing upon its broad platform, encircled by the mantle of truth, the man of God, by faith, peers into the future, withdraws the curtains of eternity, unveils the mystery of the heavens, and through the dark vista of unnumbered years, beholds the purposes of the great Elohiem, as they roll forth in all their majesty and power and glory. Thus standing upon a narrow neck of space, and beholding the past, present, and the future, he sees himself an eternal being claiming an affinity with God, a son of God, a spark of Deity struck from the fire of his eternal blaze. He looks upon the world and man, in all their various phases, knows his true interests, and with intelligence imparted by his Father Celestial, he comprehends their origin and destiny.[2]

Certainly this knowledge from the facsimiles helped Joseph Smith express in similar manner, in the twilight of his mortality, his feelings concerning the everlasting covenant. "I have witnessed the visions of eternity, and beheld the glorious mansions of bliss...have heard the voice of God, and communed with angels, and spoke as moved by the power of the Holy Ghost for the renewal of the ever-lasting covenant."[3] Through Abraham and Joseph's work, we also know that much of the mysteries of godliness and the fullness of the priesthood illustrated within the facsimiles can only be under-stood within the walls of the temple: "The Lord has ordained that all the most holy things ... all the most holy conversations and correspondence with God, angels, and spirits, shall be had only in the sanctuary of His holy Temple on the earth, when prepared for that purpose by His Saints."[4]

It thus becomes an individual stewardship for each member of "the kingdom of God on earth" to behold the great vision contained in the three facsimiles. The Dead Sea Scrolls state that "it is not only to Abraham but also to his offspring that this privilege is vouchsafed; they will be linked to God in an everlasting covenant and the Lord Himself will be their inheritance and patrimony."[5] The Lord told Oliver Cowdery through Joseph Smith how we might come to a more complete vision of the eternal plan: "Ask that you may know the mysteries of God, and ... receive knowledge from all those ancient records which have been hid up, that are sacred; and accord-ing to your faith shall it be done unto you."[6] Knowledge will come only through personal effort. Concerning the necessity of acquir-ing it during our mortal journey, it is said, speaking of the glories ahead, that "no man can enter in a moment; he must have been instructed in the government and laws ... by proper degrees, until his mind is capable ... of comprehending the propriety, justice, equality, and consistency of the same."

Joseph Smith told the Saints, "I advise all to go on to perfection and to search deeper and deeper into the mysteries of Godliness"[7] which are found within the "House of the Lord." This counsel seems so appropriate for our day. Heber C. Kimball put it somewhat more bluntly when he said,

> Many think that they are going right into the celestial kingdom of God, in their present ignorance, to at once receive glories and powers; that they are going to be Gods, while many of them

are so ignorant, that they can see or know scarcely anything. Such people talk of becoming Gods, when they do not know anything of God, or of His works; such persons have to learn repentance, and obedience to the law of God; they have got to learn to understand angels, and to comprehend and stick to the principles of this Church.[8]

In summary, Bruce R. McConkie, speaking of the Lord, said, "It is his will that we pierce the veil, rent the heavens and see visions of eternity."[9] Spiritual strength is the natural result of spiritual labor, and nothing is ever revealed without personal effort, diligence, and consistency. We are granted knowledge only when we have reached a level of righteousness, when we are ready to receive it, have the experience to understand it, and the courage to implement it. "Prove all things; hold fast that which is good."[10]

Abraham's facsimiles are part of the "mysteries, yea all the hidden mysteries of my kingdom from days of old and for ages to come" that the Lord has promised to reveal.[11] The facsimiles first of all illustrate well many principles of preparation for the ordinances of exaltation. They illustrate how knowledge and the power of God is transmitted from heaven to earth, from the sociality of heaven to covenant mortals on earth, within a circle. They portray a coronation, a bestowal of blessings and glories of God upon His covenant sons and daughters. Could this not be summarized as the rights, privileges, and blessings that are associated with the families of eternity?

May not the question Alma asked about the doctrine of Jesus Christ now be applied to the facsimiles? Is it real? Discernible? How does it taste?[12] Can we as members of The Church of Jesus Christ of Latter-day Saints echo what Joseph Smith said? "This is good doctrine. It tastes good. I can taste the principles of eternal life, and so can you. You say honey is sweet, and so do I. I can also taste the spirit of eternal life. I know it is good."[13]

President Spencer W. Kimball, in praise of father Abraham, said,

> As we follow Abraham's example, we will grow from grace to grace, we will find greater happiness and peace and rest, we will find favor with God and with man. As we follow his example, we will confirm upon ourselves and our families joy and fulfillment in this life and for all eternity.[14]

Can we now follow the declaration of the Lord? "Go ye therefore, and do the works of Abraham; enter ye into my law and ye shall be saved."[15]

Concerning the dualism within the facsimiles of the Book of Abraham, let it be said of Abraham's drawings, "Anoint thy eyes ... and wash them, ... and thou shalt see ... things which were not visible to the natural eye."[16] And of Joseph Smith, who spent a lifetime consumed in bringing forth the sacred knowledge of the ordinances of the everlasting covenant, let it be said of his explanations, "He that hath an ear, let him hear what the Spirit saith."[17] And lastly from one who has given so much about Abraham, Hugh W. Nibley, who said, "The purpose of such books [facsimiles] is not to 'prove' Mormonism to the world, but to proclaim and elucidate the universal vastness and scope of its teachings."[18]

Appendix A:
Melchizedek and Shem

A re Melchizedek and Shem the same person? Ancient biblical prophets often were identified with two or more names, and Shem was the oldest living patriarch during the time of Abraham. The Church of Jesus Christ of Latter-day Saints has more information concerning Melchizedek than any other religion. The predominant source of this knowledge came through revelations given to the prophet Joseph Smith and from translations he made of sacred writings. Melchizedek is mentioned in all four standard works because of Joseph's inspired translations.[1]

The Doctrine and Covenants tells us that the priesthood which we call "Melchizedek" was first called after the Lord and then after Enoch and today after Melchizedek: "And are priests of the Most High, after the order of Melchizedek, which was after the order of Enoch, which was after the order of the Only Begotten Son."[2] Intriguing statements as to Melchizedek's identity have been made by John Taylor, a president of The Church of Jesus Christ of Latter-day Saints; John A. Widtsoe, an apostle; and Alvin R. Dyer, a member of the First Presidency. Each claimed that Melchizedek was Shem, the son of Noah.[3] (Elder Dyer gives an interesting discourse on this subject and answers questions about the supposed two generations between them.[4]) In the Doctrine and Covenants, both Shem and Melchizedek are called "great high priest."[5]

It is interesting that the scriptures give us full details of Shem's birth and ancestry as one of Noah's sons but are silent as to Shem's ministry and later life. On the other hand, the scriptures tell of Melchizedek's ministry but give no information about his birth or ancestry. The Book of Mormon tells us that Melchizedek "was the king of Salem; and did reign under his father."[6] This statement could certainly indicate that Shem reigned under his father, Noah. In The Church of Jesus Christ of Latter-day Saints Bible Dictionary under "Shem," one is referred to "See also Melchizedek." Many nonscriptural sources equate Shem as Melchizedek. Ginsberg's Legends of the Jews states that "Shem was sometimes called Melchizedek, the king of righteousness, priest of the 'Most High God.' "[7] The Book of Jasher states, "And Adonizedek king of Jerusalem, the same was Shem."[8] Melchizedek means "King of Righteousness," while Adonizedek means "Lord of Righteousness."

Appendix B:
Abraham and Joseph

ABRAHAM

Locations: "In the land of the Chaldeans," Haran, Jershon, Shechem, Bethal, Hebron, Egypt, Bethal, Hai, Hebron, Gerar, and Beersheba.

14 yrs of age first vision. Jub. 11:18.

Jehovah: Saw or heard Jehovah over ten recorded times. Abr 1:16; Abr. 3:1; Gen. 11:29-32; Abr. 2:8; Jub. 13:4; Jub. 13:8; Abr. 2:19; Abr. 2:22; Abr. 3:11; Jub. 13:29; JST Gen. 13:13; JST Gen. 14:40; Jub. 14:18-19 and Memoirs of the Patriarchs xxi, 23-xxii, 26; JST Gen. 15:1, 9-12; JST Gen. 17:1; Jub. 15:5; Gen. 17:9; Gen. 22:14, 17-18; Jub. 18:14-16.

JOSEPH

Locations: Sharon, Manchester, Palmyra Harmony, Fayette, Kirtland, Hiram, Independence, Far West, Liberty, Ramus, and Nauvoo.

14 yrs of age first vision. JS-H 1:17.

Jesus Christ: Saw or heard Jesus Christ ten recorded times. JS-H: 1:17; D&C 6:36-37; HC 1:76; D&C 27; D&C 76:12, 14, 21, 23; A. H. Cannon Journal, 25 Aug. 1880; D&C 137:3; HC 2:383; D&C 110:2-4; HC 3:388.

Seer: "And I, Abraham, had the Urim and Thummim, which the Lord my God had given unto me, in Ur of the Chaldees." Abr. 3:1.

Priesthood: "Behold, I will lead thee by my hand, and I will take thee, to put upon thee my name, even the Priesthood of thy father, and my power shall be over thee." Abr. 1:18;"Which Abraham received the priesthood from Melchizedek, who received it through the lineage of his fathers, even till Noah." D&C 84:14;"God blessed Abram, ... according to the blessing wherewith Melchizedek had blessed him." JST Gen. 14:40; Became God's High Priest, Abr. 1: 2.

Records: Abraham keeper of the records; the "Book of Remembrance" (Abr. 1:28), of Adam (Moses 6:8), of Enoch (Moses 6:46, D&C 107:57), and of others (Moses 6:5) and added his records to them (Abr. 1:31).

Jails: Kardi and Kutha, Mesopòtamia.

See Nibley, Hugh, "A New Look at the Pearl of Great Price," *Era*, April 1969, p. 67.

Seer: "Now, behold, I say unto you, that because you delivered up those writings which you had power given unto you to translate by the means of the Urim and Thummim..." D&C 10:1.

Priesthood: "Upon you my fellow servants, in the name of Messiah I confer the Priesthood of Aaron..." D&C 13:1;

"And also with Peter, and James, and John, whom I have sent unto you, by whom I have ordained you and confirmed you to be apostles, and especial witnesses of my name, and bear the keys of your ministry and of the same things which I revealed unto them ... " D&C 27:12; Became God's High Priest, D&C 107:22.

Records: "Behold, thou wast called and chosen to write the Book of Mormon..." D&C 24:1; "And I have given unto him the keys of the mystery of those things which have been sealed..." D&C 35:18; Old and New Testament, D&C 45:60-61.

Jails: Richmond, Liberty, and Gallatin, MO, and Carthage, IL. See Cottle, Thomas D. and Patricia C., *Liberty Jail and the Legacy of Joseph.*

Temple: "In the mount of the Lord it shall be seen..." Gen. 22:14.

Temple: "And I will show unto my servant Joseph all things pertaining to this house [temple] and the priesthood thereof ... " D&C 124:42.

Celestial Kingdom (Premortal): "Now the Lord had shown unto me, Abraham, the intelligences that were organized before the world was; and among all these there were many of the noble and great ones ... " Abr. 3:22.

Celestial Kingdom (Postmortal): "The heavens were opened upon us, and I beheld the celestial kingdom of God, and the glory thereof..." D&C 137:1.

Fullness: "Abraham ... as Isaac also and Jacob did none other things than that which they were commanded; and because they did none other things than that which they were commanded, they have entered into their exaltation, according to the promises, and sit upon thrones, and are not angels but are gods." D&C 132:37.

Fullness: On 28 September 1843, four months after their sealing, Joseph Smith Jr. and Emma Hale Smith were the first in this dispensation to receive the fullness of the priesthood. See Cottle and Cottle, Liberty Jail and the Legacy of Joseph, p. 172, citing The Words of Joseph Smith, comp. & ed. Ehat & Cook, 294, 303-4; D&C 132:49.

Burial: Beside Sarah in cave of the field of Ephron-Machpelah at Hebron.

Burial: Beside Emma in the family cemetery at Nauvoo, Illinois.

Appendix C:
Hypocephali

Figure 1
(Ldy Ta-khred-Khonsu, Ashmolean 1982-1095)

Figure 2

Figure 3
(3 PSBA, 8 March 1911)

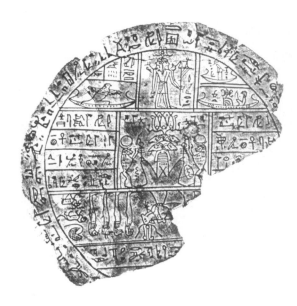

Figure 4
(Lady Wst-wrt, Vienna 253 a/2)

Figure 5

Figure 6
(Henry Meux from Thebes)

Figure 7
(Gold Leaf, Louvre N3524)

Figure 8
(Cha–Kheper, Louvre E26834a)

Appendix D:
Two Equal Powers and Capacities

The Godhead declare through scriptures and prophets that female and male are equal. This total equality is inherent to the term god, which literally incorporates both genders; hence, the declaration that male and female were created in the likeness of God. The male and female, with their individual powers and capacities, have different responsibilities and assignments in the eternal plan of salvation. Throughout this eternity, as within all eternities, this principle has been and always will be true. The foundation of every society that has ever existed has been the union of male and female. The Kabbalah says, "For they could not permanently exist save in another aspect of the Male and the Female (their countenances being joined together)," as "Chokmah is the Father, and Binah is the Mother, ... understanding counterbalanced together is most perfect equality of Male and Female."[1]

The false tradition of inequality between male and female within world cultures stemmed from the influence of the ancient, almost world-dominant, King Ahasuerus. His destructive degree of inequality of the genders was precipitated by his wife Queen Vashti.[2] This tradition of inequality made its way into world customs and, because of this, even into the minds of some members of the Church throughout its history. In recent years strong efforts have come forth through Church leadership declaration, correspondence, and proclamation to fortify the truth of total equality of man and woman, including the 1978 Official Declaration—2, the official 1990 correspondence to temple presidents and, of course, the 1995 proclamation on the family. On September 23, 1995, President Gordon B. Hinckley read that proclamation. It begins,

> We, the First Presidency and the Council of the Twelve Apostles of The Church of Jesus Christ of Latter-day Saints [fifteen prophets, seers, and revelators of God], solemnly proclaim that marriage between a man and a woman is ordained of God and that the family is central to the Creator's plan for the eternal destiny of His children.
>
> All human beings—male and female—are created in the image of God. Each is a beloved spirit son or daughter of heavenly parents, and, as such, each has a divine nature and destiny. Gender is an essential characteristic of individual premortal, mortal, and eternal identity and purpose.[3]

While the absolute equality of male and female is true, each works under a mandate of responsibility indicative of their eternal power and capacity. For the male, his priesthood stewardship is summarized as follows:

> Verily, if a man be called of my Father, as was Aaron, by mine own voice, and by the voice of him that sent me, and I have endowed him with the keys of the power of this priesthood, if he do anything in my name, and according to my law and by my word, he will not commit sin, and I will justify him.[4]

For the female, her creative stewardship is summarized as being

> to multiply and replenish the earth, according to my commandment, and to fulfil the promise which was given by my Father before the foundation of the world, and for their

exaltation in the eternal worlds, that they may bear the souls of men; for herein is the work of my Father continued, that he may be glorified.[5]

This principle was understood by Adam and Eve and is evidenced within the scriptures. The Book of Abraham and D&C 132, as quoted above, are some of our strongest scriptural sources that teach of these two powers coming together with their separate responsibilities to reach the measure of their creation. (See Facsimiles 2 and 3.) The earth line of the second facsimile of Abraham demonstrates the male receiving power from heaven and the female as the source of creative power. The third facsimile shows the coronation of the two equal capacities into the royalty of godhood. First Samuel 2:1 and 10 are scriptural illustrations of the two powers, creative and priesthood, using the symbolism of horns. The Lord gives as the reason for the Flood the adulteration of these two responsibilities. When Noah, as recorded in Moses 8:15, asks the Lord why He will flood the earth, Noah is told that those of one power "sell themselves" and the other power "no longer hearkens" to authority.

Additional reference: Talmage, James E., "The Eternity of Sex," Young Women's Journal, October 1914, pp. 600-604.

Appendix E:
Angels of God

John the beloved apostle saw in vision the latter days when four destroying angels would bring judgments upon the inhabitants of the earth. John then beheld another angel ascending from the east, having the seal of the living God, who said: "Hurt not the earth, neither the sea, nor the trees, till we have sealed the servants of our God in their foreheads."[1] As evidence of these great angels being held back until the sealing can be accomplished throughout the entire earth, consider President Ezra Taft Benson's pleading that these destroying angels be held back in his final comments of the April 1986 General Conference. As Joseph Smith sought to understand the revelation of John, he too was given a revelation, which is found in Doctrine and Covenants section 77, verses 8-9. Joseph later elaborated on this.

> Four destroying angels holding power over the four quarters of the earth until the servants of God are sealed in their foreheads, which signifies sealing the blessing upon their heads, meaning the everlasting covenant, thereby making their calling and election sure. When a seal is put upon the father and mother, it secures their posterity, so that they cannot be lost, but will be saved by virtue of the covenant of their father and mother.[2]

Elder Orson F. Whitney further enlarged on the subject.

> The Prophet Joseph Smith never taught more comforting doctrine—that the eternal sealings of faithful parents and the divine promises made to them ... would save not only themselves, but likewise their posterity. Though some of the sheep may wander, the eye of the Shepherd is upon them, and sooner or later they will feel the tentacles of Divine Providence reaching out after them and drawing them back to the fold. Either in this life or the life to come, they will return.[3]

Brother Packer also addressed this subject in the April 1992 General Conference, speaking on "The measure of a successful parent." After quoting the above statements he said,

> We cannot overemphasize the value of temple marriage, the binding ties of the sealing ordinance, and the standards of worthiness required of them. When parents keep the covenants they have made at the altar of the temple, their children will be forever bound to them. President Brigham Young said: 'Let the father and mother, who are members of this Church and Kingdom, take a righteous course, and strive with all their might never to do a wrong, but to do good all their lives; if they have one child or one hundred children, if they conduct themselves towards them as they should, binding them to the Lord by their faith and prayers, I care not where those children go, they are bound up to their parents by an everlasting tie, and no power of earth or hell can separate them from their parents in eternity; they will return again to the fountain from whence they sprang.'[4]

By keeping an eye open one will quickly see that the symbolism of four angels is very prevalent in the world cultures of today.

Appendix F:
An Eternity

Abraham understood that eternities are the work of the Gods, the patriarchal order of exalted fathers,[1] and are sequential in the form of one eternal round without beginning and without end.[2] The eternal progression of man, even one eternal round,[3] new heaven and new earth,[4] can also be described as "from eternity to eternity."[5] Abraham also knew that each eternity has a period of accomplishment, completion, or fulfillment. William W. Phelps, David Hyrum Smith, and Bruce R. McConkie, at various times, have said that the length of an eternity is 2,555,000,000 years.[6] Facsimile No. 2 could be a source of their information, beginning with the statement that "one day in Kolob is equal to a thousand years according to the measurement of this earth."[7] We need only multiply 1000 by 365 days of the year, times 7000 (the temporal portion of the earth's existence), to arrive at the number 2,555,000,000. It is interesting that a secular discovery in 1999, having to do with shale in Australia, has altered the scientific community's theory about the age of the earth. With this recent finding, the earth's age of existence is now purported to be 2,700,000,000 years old.[8] This is surprisingly close to information revealed by Phelps, Smith, and McConkie, the foundation for which was father Abraham, and through Abraham to the prophet Joseph Smith.

Adam certainly learned during the Creation that the composite of all eternities are infinite, without beginning and without end, but the physical or mortal composition of each is not eternal. All entities in the mortal stage are subject to death, decay, or disintegration in some form; therefore, all physical forms of animal, vegetable, and mineral at the completion of mortality must be glorified in order to become eternal. Understanding Father in heaven's plan of salvation, Adam and Eve realized that when the stage of glorification is reached, each entity will become immortal and eternal[9] with capabilities of perpetuation into the next eternity, which is the ultimate fulfillment of God's work and glory. This entire concept has been beautifully summarized by Orson Pratt.

> But there is another thing I want you to understand. This will not be kept up to all eternity, it is merely a preparation for something still greater. And what is that? By and by, when each of these creations has fulfilled the measure and bounds set and the times given for its continuance in a temporal state, it and its inhabitants who are worthy will be made celestial and glorified together. Then, from that time henceforth and for ever, there will be no intervening veil between God and his people who are sanctified and glorified, and he will not be under the necessity of withdrawing from one to go and visit another, because they will all be in his presence. It matters not how far in space these creations may be located from any special celestial kingdom where the Lord our God shall dwell, they will be able to see him at all times. Why? Because it is only the fall, and the veil that has been shut down over this creation, that keep us from the presence of God. Let the veil be removed, which now hinders us from beholding the glory of God and the celestial kingdom; let this creation be once perfected, after having passed through its various ordeals, after having enjoyed the light of the countenance of our Lord, in our hour and in our season, and let all things be perfected and glorified, and there will be no necessity for this veil being shut down.[1]

Appendix G:
Bible and Civilization Chronology

The theological community agrees that the time of Adam and Eve cannot accurately be dated. Most feel that accurate Bible dates begin with the period of the Judges, 1200–1050 B.C. This accuracy certainly increases with every succeeding century as synchronisms with secular history become available. The chronology of 4000 B.C. most often used for the entrance of Adam and Eve into the Garden of Eden is usually attributed to Archbishop James Ussher from Armagh, Ireland. In 1654 his two-volume work, Annales Veteris et Novi Tetamenti (Annals of the Ancient and New Testaments), was published and projected 4004 B.C. as the origin of creation. A contemporary of Ussher, John Lightfoot of Cambridge University, reaffirmed this, giving the month and time.[1] This date continues to be used even though archeological evidence shows many great civilizations originated in China, Egypt, India, Mesopotamia, and other locations that provide a genealogy of their kings dating back near this time. This chronology, however, is rarely taken seriously by Bible scholars. The LDS Bible Dictionary, page 635, under "Chronology" states, "The dates found at the top of many printed English Bibles are due to Archbishop Ussher. Some of them have been shown to be incorrect."

The starting point becomes extremely important, for if the date for Adam and Eve is wrong, the entire time span between Adam and Eve and the Judges is incorrect. Glenn A. Scott gives a tremendous treatise on this in which two findings that collaborate one another support the premise that the Flood was much earlier, possibly 4000 B.C.[2] Archaeological findings at Ur, Kish, Erech, Shuruppak, Lagash, and Nineveh all show a deep layer of silt, between eight and ten feet thick, under the cities. The British archaeologist Professor C. Leonard Woolley, at Ur in 1929, "found indisputable evidences of a flood in the neighborhood of Abraham's ancestral city"[3] which indicates this silt represented "a sudden and drastic break in the continuity of history."[4] Silt of this magnitude provides strong evidence for a worldwide flood, which Werner Keller dates at 4000 B.C.

Concerning the world's first civilizations, J. Mellaart stated, "let us say 5000 B.C., we find throughout the greater part of the Near East ... villages, market towns ... and castles of local rulers" widely in touch with each other as "goods and raw materials were traded over great distances."[5] Early Mesopotamian, Egyptian, Cretian, Indian, Chinese, and American civilizations fit closely with this same time frame.[6] In the discipline of archeology we see "Jericho by general consensus the oldest city in the world." The digs at this city show "it emerges abruptly full-blown, with a sophisticated and stereotyped architecture that remains unchanged for twenty-one successive town-levels."[7] Other evidences that the appearance of Adam and Eve may have been earlier is that the first languages of the world—Egyptian, Sumerian, and dialects of India—originated much sooner.

The almost simultaneous appearance of multiple civilizations, the surfacing of multiple languages, both at a much earlier time than Ussher's chronology, suggests evidences that the Flood, not the happenings in the Garden of Eden, took place about 4000 B.C. Calculating by the biblical genealogies, which total one thousand six hundred and fifty years, and adding this to 4000 B.C. (time of the Flood) would put the entrance of Adam and Eve in the garden at about 5700 B.C. The Book of Mormon, believed to be the most correct book on earth, cites an interesting verse that implies a much longer period between Adam and the mortal life of Jesus Christ than the chronology used today indicates.

> Yea, and behold I say unto you, that Abraham not only knew of these things, but there were many before the days of Abraham who were called by the order of God; yea, even after the order of his Son; and this that it should be shown unto the people, a great many thousand years before his coming, that even redemption should come unto them.[8]

Notes

(See Bibliography for full citations)

Introduction

1. Jedediah M. Grant, *Journal of Discourses*, 4:126; hereafter JD.

2. George Q. Cannon, JD 12:46.

3. Joseph Smith, *Teachings of the Prophet Joseph Smith*, 190; hereafter TPJS.

4. Brother Nibley's volumes of work on this subject has expanded over fifty years. A list of his works can be obtained from the Foundation for Ancient Research and Mormon Studies (FARMS) at Brigham Young University, P.O. Box 7113, University Station, Provo, UT 84602; Michael Dennis Rhodes, "A Translation and Commentary of the Joseph Smith Hypocephalus," *Brigham Young University (BYU) Studies* 17 no. 3 (1977); H. Donl Peterson, *The Story of the Book of Abraham*; Jay M. Todd, *The Saga of the Book of Abraham*, and "Papyri, Joseph Smith" in *Encyclopedia of Mormonism* vol. 3, 1058-1060; and John A. Gee, *A History of the Joseph Smith Papyri and Book of Abraham*, and Stephen D. Rick, ed., "Eyewitness, Hearsay, and Physical Evidence of the Joseph Smith Papyri," in *The Disciple as Witness*.

5. Luke 16:22, 30-31.

6.   1 Nephi 15:14

7.   Doctrine & Covenants 132 (hereafter D&C); Abraham 1:2;
       2:9–11; Explanations of Facsimile no. 2.

Chapter 1: Father Abraham

1.   Abraham 3:22.

2.   Abraham 3:23; D&C 132:11.

3.   Jasher 7:20 and 50 fn. The book of Jasher can be found in
       Albinus Alcuin, trans., *The Book of Jasher*; hereafter Jasher.

4.   Jubilees 11:14–15. The book of Jubilees can be found in
       James H. Charlesworth, *The Old Testament Pseudepigrapha*
       vol. 2, 35–142; hereafter Jubilees.

5.   The birth of Abraham cannot be fixed with accuracy. Was
       Abraham fifty-eight years old or five years old when Noah
       died? Either can be calculated by working existing figures.
       Any date set for Abraham could still be faulty, for it is based
       on dates ascribed to Adam and Eve, which could have been
       much earlier. What we do know is that Genesis 11:26 says
       "and Terah lived seventy years, and begat Abram, Nahor and
       Haran." Abraham was the youngest of the brothers. Genesis
       12:4 states that Abram was seventy-six years old when he
       left Haran after his father Terah died. And Abraham states in
       his record (Abraham 3:14) that he left Haran when he was
       sixty-two years old, and his father Terah was still alive and
       living there. Dr. Nibley discusses this in his book *Abraham
       in Egypt*, 115–118.

6.   In 1654 Archbishop James Ussher's two-volume work,
       Annales Veteris et Novi Tetamenti (Annals of the Ancient
       and New Testaments) was published and projected 4004 B.C.
       as the origin of creation. (As seen in Glenn A. Scott, *Voices
       from the Dust: New Light on an Ancient American Record*, 9.)
       A contemporary of Ussher, John Lightfoot of Cambridge
       University, reaffirmed this, giving the month and time.

This date continues to be used, even though archeological
evidence shows many great civilizations originated in China,
Egypt, India, Mesopotamia, and other locations with kings
whose genealogies date back near this time. This chronology,
however, is rarely taken seriously by Bible scholars. The
LDS Bible Dictionary, 635, under "Chronology," states, "The
dates found at the top of many printed English Bibles
are due to Archbishop Ussher. Some of them have been
shown to be incorrect." Henry Halley states in his Bible
Handbook, "Ussher's guesses are based on false premises and
the genealogies of Genesis are undoubtedly abbreviated."
This becomes extremely important, for if the date for Adam
and Eve is wrong, the entire timetable is incorrect. The Book
of Mormon, believed to be the most correct book on earth,
sites an interesting verse that implies a much longer period
between Adam and the mortal life of Jesus Christ than the
chronology used today indicates. "Yea, and behold I say unto
you, that Abraham not only knew of these things, but there
were many before the days of Abraham who were called by
the order of God; yea, even after the order of his Son; and
this that it should be shown unto the people, a great many
thousand years before his coming, that even redemption
should come unto them." Is it any wonder then that Dr.
Nibley says, "We have a range of two thousand years in
which the experts are seeking to find an exact date for
Abraham." (From page 53 of his 1981 book, Nibley, *Abraham
in Egypt*.)

7.   Hugh Nibley, "There Were Jaredites," *Improvement Era* 59,
      1956, 710; hereafter Era.

8.   Genesis 11:27–28.

9.   *The LDS Bible Dictionary*, 610 states, "By this word is
      generally meant those sacred books of the Jewish people
      which were not included in the Hebrew Bible." See D&C
      91 for prophetic instructions concerning the Apocrypha.

10.   Jasher 8:35–36.

11. Jasher 9:5-6; 11:13.

12. Alvin R. Dyer, *The Lord Speaketh*, 286.

13. *The LDS Bible Dictionary*, 755 states: "The word refers to certain noncanonical writings purported to have come from biblical characters, and refers to books of ancient Jewish literature outside the canon and the apocrypha."

14. Jubilees 12:12.

15. Abraham 1:20.

16. Abraham 1:10.

17. *Ensign*, September 1980, 33.

18. Hugh Nibley, "A New Look at the Pearl of Great Price," *Era* 71-73, April 1969, 66-69.

19. Abraham 1:5.

20. Abraham 1:17.

21. Abraham 1:9, 11.

22. Abraham 1:13-14.

23. Abraham 1:4.

24. Abraham 1:15.

25. Abraham 1:18.

26. Abraham 3:1.

27. Abraham 4 & 5.

28. Abraham 1:31.

29. Mosiah 8:13, 15-16.

30. D&C 21:1.

31. D&C 121:29-32.

32. Abraham 3. This concept is explained beautifully by Alma the Younger in Alma 13.

33. TPJS, 308.

34. D&C 107:2-3.

35. Joseph Smith, *The Words of Joseph Smith*, 245; hereafter WJS.

36. Sidney B. Sperry, "Abraham's Three Visitors," found in the Editorial Note by James E. Talmage, *Era*, August 1931, 585.

37. *Encyclopedia of Mormonism*, 1:8.

38. Joseph Smith Translation Genesis 14:32-33 (hereafter JST); N.B. Lundwall, *A Compilation Containing the Lectures on Faith*, 29.

39. Genesis 14:18.

40. TPJS, 322-23.

41. D&C 107:52.

42. Abraham 1: 2.

43. Abraham 1:1-2.

44. Alma 13:17-18.

45. JST Genesis 14:40.

46. Abraham 2:15.

47. Abraham 2:2; Jasher 12:44-45.

48. Genesis 17:17; Jasher 9:4.

49. Nibley, "A New Look at the Pearl of Great Price," *Era*, April 1969, 68.

50. *Era*, April 1970, 79-95.

51. Jasher 15:14.

52. William Whiston, *The Works of Flavius Josephus*, 32.

53. Theodor H. Gaster, *The Dead Sea Scriptures*, 364-65.

54. Genesis 21:12, cf. Genesis 16:4-6.

55. Genesis 20.

56. Jasher 15:24.

57.   Jasher 20:13.

58.   Gaster, *The Dead Sea Scriptures*, 366; *Encyclopedia of Mormonism*, 1:8.

59.   Genesis 20:17–18.

60.   Abraham 2:4.

61.   Abraham 2:6.

62.   Abraham 2:8.

63.   Abraham 2:15.

64.   Abraham 2:10–11.

65.   Abraham 2:9–11; WJS, 303.

66.   Abraham 2:6.

67.   Abraham 2:16 fn. c.

68.   Joshua 15:22.

69.   1 Kings 16:8.

70.   Genesis 12:6.

71.   Abraham 2:18–19.

72.   Jubilees 13:6–8.

73.   Abraham 2:21; Genesis 12:10.

74.   Abraham 2:23–24.

75.   Abraham 3:15.

76.   Abraham 1:26–27.

77.   Jubilees 13:11–12.

78.   Whiston, *The Works of Flavius Josephus*, 32.

79.   Abraham 1:21; Genesis 9:22, 10:6.

80.   Nibley, "A New Look at the Pearl of Great Price," *Era*, April 1969, 69; Jubilees 13:12.

81.   Genesis 12:16.

82. Genesis 13:3-4; Jubilees 13:15; Jasher 15:34; Gaster, *The Dead Sea Scriptures*, 367-68.

83. Genesis 13:18.

84. Jasher 15:47.

85. Gaster, *The Dead Sea Scriptures*, 372.

86. W. Cleon Skousen, *The First 2,000 Years*, 265.

87. Genesis 17:5, 15; Jubilees 15:5-7, 15-16.

88. Genesis 12:2.

89. Jubilees 14:20.

90. Genesis 17:1.

91. JST Genesis 17:11; Jubilees 15:23-25.

92. Hebrews 7:1-2.

93. Jasher 16:11-12.

94. WJS, 246.

95. John Taylor, JD 17:207, as seen in Richard Ware, "The Holy Priesthood." See Part II, From Adam to Jethro.

96. D&C 132:19.

97. As seen in Ware, "The Holy Priesthood," 18.

98. Genesis 15:5.

99. TPJS, 322-23.

100. Abraham 1:2.

101. JST Genesis 25:12.

102. 2 Peter 1:17-19.

103. John Taylor, "The John Taylor Nauvoo Journal", Dean C. Jessee, ed., *BYU Studies* 23, no. 3 (1983): 56.

104. Genesis 17:19; Galatians, 4:28; Hebrews 11:9, 20.

105. Abraham 1:25-26, 31.

106. Genesis 12:2–3; 18:17–19.

107. Abraham 2:11.

108. Genesis 1:28; Moses 3:22–24.

109. 1 Nephi 15:18; Acts 3:25.

110. This is outlined in the *LDS Bible Dictionary* under "Abraham, Covenant of," 602.

111. For the sequence of our dispensation read Thomas D. Cottle, chapter 10, "Doctrines to Its Fullness", *Liberty Jail and the Legacy of Joseph.*

112. TPJS, 32.

113. Daniel Tyler, "Temples," *Juvenile Instructor*, May 15, 1880, 111.

114. D&C 132:34, 65.

115. Galatians 3:26–29.

116. Genesis 22:17.

117. Matthew 8:1–17.

118. TPJS, 150.

119. Genesis 20:2; Jubilees 17:17.

120. *Bible Lands Posters Commentary*, 13.

121. Genesis 21:33; Isaiah 40:28; Romans 16:26; D&C 133:34.

122. Genesis 18:10.

123. Genesis 22:2.

124. Jacob 4:5.

125. TPJS, 322.

126. D&C 84:38.

127. D&C 84:34–38; Joseph Smith, *History of The Church of Jesus Christ of Latter-day Saints*, 5:2; hereafter HC.

128. Genesis 49:10, 22–26.

129. Genesis 25:12–16.

130. Genesis 25:1–7.

131. D&C 124:58.

132. 1 Nephi 17:40; 2 Nephi 29:14; 3 Nephi 20:25; Mormon 5:20.

133. D&C 107:19.

134. Cottle, *Liberty Jail and the Legacy of Joseph.* See chapter 2, "The Messengers of the Fullness," and D&C 128:21.

135. JD 21:94.

136. Cottle, *Liberty Jail and the Legacy of Joseph*, 14–15.

137. TPJS, 322–23.

138. Abraham 4:1; TPJS, 349.

139. Abraham; Jubilees 11:18; Joseph Smith–History 1:17; hereafter JS-H.

140. Nibley, "A New Look at the Pearl of Great Price," *Era*, April 1969, 67.

141. Abraham 1:2.

142. D&C 121:26–27.

143. TPJS, 322.

144. D&C 132:37.

145. D&C 132:29–50; Abraham 2:9–11.

Chapter 2: The Book of Abraham

1.   Malachi 4:5–6.

2.   D&C 2:3.

3.   Hugh Nibley, "As Things Stand at the Moment," *BYU Studies* 9, no. 1 (1969): 78.

4.   Abraham 1:26.

5.   Hugh Nibley, "Fragment Found in Salt Lake City," *BYU Studies* 8, no. 2 (1968): 192.

6.   HC 2:235.

7.   Gee, Appendix, "The Joseph Smith Papyri: Then and Now," *A History of the Joseph Smith Papyri and Book of Abraham*, 2.

8.   James R. Clark, "Joseph Smith and the Lobolo Egyptian Papyri," *BYU Studies* 8 no. 2 (1968): 196.

9.   Hugh Nibley, "I Have a Question," *Ensign*, March 1976, 34.

10. Gee, *A History of the Joseph Smith Papyri and Book of Abraham*, 7.

11. Peterson, *The Story of the Book of Abraham*, 158.

12. Gee, *A History of the Joseph Smith Papyri and Book of Abraham*, 11 & fig 7.

13. Hugh Nibley, "The Meaning of the Kirtland Egyptian Papers," *BYU Studies* 11, no. 4 (1971): 351, 355.

14. D&C 121:26.

15. Cottle, chapter 10, "Doctrine to Its Fullness," *Liberty Jail and the Legacy of Joseph*.

16. HC 2:235–36, 334, 348–51.

17. HC 2:388.

18. 1 Nephi 1:2.

19. Era, 45:529, as seen in Nibley, "The Meaning of The Kirtland Egyptian Papers," *BYU Studies* 11, no. 2 (1971): 358.

20. Nibley, "As Things Stand at the Moment," *BYU Studies* 9, no. 1 (1969): 78.

21. D&C 110:12.

22. Genesis 12:2.

23. 1 Nephi 15:18.

24. John 8:38–39.

25. D&C 132:32.

26. 1 Nephi 13:34.

27. Hugh Nibley, *Old Testament and Related Studies* vol. 1, 68; D&C 93:30.

28. John Taylor, *The Mormon 1*, no. 23 as seen in John Taylor, *The Gospel Kingdom*, 3.

29. Hugh Nibley, "Fragment Found in Salt Lake City", *BYU Studies* 8, no. 2 (1968), 193; HC 2:286.

30. Joseph Smith, "The King Follett Discourse 'A Newly Amalgamated Text,'" *BYU Studies* 18, no. 2 (1977): 201.

31. HC 4:519.

32. D&C 132:3.

33. D&C 132:7.

34. D&C 132:20, 37.

35. JS-H 1:19.

36. TPJS, 325.

37. D&C 84:34.

38. Galatians 3:29.

Chapter 3: The Everlasting Covenant

1. JD 24:173.

2. Erastus Snow, JD 24:161.

3. TPJS, 190.

4. Alma 34:13-15.

5. Joseph F. Smith, *Gospel Doctrine*, 100.

6. 1 Peter 1:2; Abraham 3:22-24; Romans 9, heading in LDS Bible.

7. *Melchizedek Priesthood Manual*, 1973-74, 27, 49.

8. D&C 132:3, 48.

9.   D&C 132:7.

10. D&C 66:2; Moses 6:61-62.

11. Hebrews 9:14-15.

12. D&C 1:22-23 & 15.

13. D&C 136:4.

14. Moses 6:52-53.

15. 2 Nephi 9:21; Mosiah 4:7; Mormon 3:20. Members of the Church need not be concerned with speculation about Pre-Adamites.

16. Adam: Moses 5:4-10.

     Enoch: JST Genesis 9:21-15; Moses 6:26-27; Genesis 5:24.

     Noah: Moses 8:19-27; Genesis 8:20-9:20.

     Abraham: Abraham 1:2-4, 15-19; 2:6-13, 17-18; 3:5; Genesis 11:28-32; 12:6-8; 15; 17:1-22; 21:33; 22:9-18.

     Isaac: Genesis 26:2-5, 23-25.

     Jacob: Genesis 28:10-22; 32:24-32.

     Moses: Exodus 19-24.

17. Ezekiel 37:26.

18. 2 Nephi 31:17-21.

19. Following the format of doctrine from the keys that were restored at the Kirtland Temple on April 3, 1836, the three goals we now know as the threefold mission of the Church were first established and declared by the early brethren and formalized by President Spencer W. Kimball at the April 1981 General Conference. They are (1) To proclaim the gospel of the Lord Jesus Christ to every nation, kindred, tongue, and people; (2) To perfect the Saints by preparing them to receive the ordinances of the gospel and by instruction and discipline to gain exaltation; (3) To redeem the dead by performing vicarious ordinances of the gospel for those who have lived on the earth.

20. Matthew 4:48 fn. a & b.

21. D&C 131:1-4; 84:37-39.

22. Abraham 1:2.

23. Cottle, *Liberty Jail and the Legacy of Joseph*, 171-172.

24. D&C 84:20-21.

25. D&C 132:6; 133:57.

26. Moses 1:39.

27. D&C 121:27; 128:21.

28. Isaiah 55:3.

29. Galatians 3:7-9.

30. D&C 66:2.

31. George Q. Cannon, *Gospel Truth*, 330; *Juvenile Instructor* 30, January 15, 1895, 55-56.

32. D&C 90:11.

33. Isaiah 11:9.

34. D&C 98:14-15.

35. D&C 136:4.

36. Boyd K. Packer, *The Holy Temple*, 171.

Chapter 4: Three Facsimiles

1. Nibley, "I Have a Question," *Ensign*, March 1976, 34.

2. Mormon 9:32.

3. Explanation Facsimile No. 3.

4. Nibley, "A New Look at the Pearl of Great Price," *Era*, November 1968, 40.

5. Abraham 1:12, 14.

6.   Nibley, "A New Look at the Pearl of Great Price," *Era*, March 1969, 84.

7.   E. A. Wallis Budge, *The Gods of the Egyptians*, 1:323.

8.   Budge, *The Gods of the Egyptians*, 1:322.

9.   Samuel Birch, " Hypocephalus in the British Museum No 8445f," *Proceedings for the Society of Biblical Archaeology*, 6 May 1884, 185, as seen in Rhodes, "A Translation and Commentary of the Joseph Smith Hypocephalus," *BYU Studies* 17, no. 3 (1977): 267.

10. Latter Day Saints' *Messenger and Advocate* vol. II, no. 3, December 1835, 236.

11. 3 Nephi 27:10.

12. D&C 93:24.

13. D&C 121:26, 33.

14. For example see Explanation Facsimile No. 2, Fig. 8.

15. Hugh Nibley, "What Is 'The Book of Breathings?'" *BYU Studies* 11, no. 2 (1971): 186.

16. D&C 124:40–43; italics added.

17. 1 Nephi 6:4–5.

Chapter 5: Facsimile No. 1

1.   Abraham 1:7–11.

2.   George Q. Cannon, *Conference Report,* April, 1899, 66; hereafter CR.

3.   CR, October 1900, 2.

4.   Omni 1:26.

5.   D&C 121:36.

6.   Abraham 1:15–16.

7.   1 Nephi 12:17.

8.   E.H. Anderson, "The Book of the Revelation of Abraham,"
     Era 1, 794-795.

9.   Archaeologia vol. iii. 'The Papyrus of Nesi-Amsu,' as seen in
     Budge, *The Gods of the Egyptians*, 1:325-328.

10. Nibley, "A New Look at the Pearl of Great Price," *Era*,
     August 1969, 81.

11. Doyle G. Green, "New Light on Joseph Smith's Egyptian
     Papyri," *Era*, February 1968, 40.

12. Nibley, "A New Look at the Pearl of Great Price," *Era*,
     September 1968, 66; and Nibley, "As Things Stand at the
     Moment," *BYU Studies* 9, no. 1 (1969): 83.

13. D&C 129:1-2; TPJS, 170, 191, & 325.

14. D&C 84:47-48.

15. Alma 12:28-29.

16. Cottle, chapter 2, "The Messengers of the Fullness," in *Liberty
     Jail and the Legacy of Joseph*.

17. Malachi 3: heading.

18. Moroni 7:31.

19. Abraham 1:15.

20. Abraham 2:13.

21. Anderson, "The Book of the Revelation of Abraham," *Era*
     1, 713.

22. Nibley, "A New Look at the Pearl of Great Price," *Era*, July
     1969, 108.

23. Nibley, "A New Look at the Pearl of Great Price," *Era*,
     August 1969, 77.

24. Parley P. Pratt, "Spiritual Communication," discourse
     delivered at the laying of the northeast cornerstone of the
     Salt Lake Temple, April 6, 1853 as seen in N. B. Lundwall,
     Temples of the Most High, 142, 144.

25. D&C 132:20, 37; 137:5; Book of Abraham, Facsimile 2, Fig. 3; and Pratt, "Spiritual Communication," in *Temples of the Most High*, 143.

26. WJS, 246.

27. Lamentations 3:41.

28. Abraham 1:16.

29. Hugh Nibley, Era, May 1956, 334 scriptural ref.

30. Reference to upraised hands as here in the Pearl of Great Price is also found in the other books of the scriptures. Old Testament: 1 Kings 8:22–55; Exodus 9:33. New Testament: Luke 24:50. Book of Mormon: Alma 5:19. D&C: 88:120, 109:9.

31. Ezekiel 47:14 fn.; Psalms 119:48.

32. D&C 88: 132.

33. Exodus 17:11–15.

34. 1 Kings 8:21.

35. Nehemiah 8:6.

36. Luke 24:50.

37. D&C 88: 120.

38. Psalms 24:3–4.

39. Job 11:13.

40. 3 Nephi 27:9.

41. TPJS, 350.

42. Ether 3:20.

43. JD 14:157.

44. Abraham 1:7.

45. D&C 121:4.

46. Abraham 3:28.

47. JD 1:334.

48. 2 Nephi 2:11.

49. Mormon 1:19.

50. Abraham 1:20.

51. D&C 84:20.

52. Acts 5:36.

53. Revelation 8:3.

54. Bruce R. McConkie, *Mormon Doctrine*, 21.

55. Exodus 40:29.

56. Exodus 30:6.

57. Revelation 9:13.

58. Moses 5:5–6; D&C 131:2.

59. Abraham 3:25–26.

60. D&C 101:4.

61. D&C 98:11–13.

62. D&C 124:55.

63. Lundwall, *A Compilation Containing the Lectures on Faith*, 6:7.

64. D&C 132:50.

65. D&C 98:14.

66. Anderson, "The Book of the Revelation of Abraham," *Era* 1, 797.

67. *Era*, September 1969, 85–86.

68. *Era*, September 1969, 59, 68–69.

69. *Era*, August 1969, 81.

70. *Era*, September 1969, 85.

71. Nibley, "A New Look at the Pearl of Great Price," *Era*, August 1969, 82.

72. Abraham 1:13.

73. Robert C. Webb, *Smith as a Translator*, 144.

74. Revelation 7:1-3.

75. D&C 77:8.

76. Louis Ginsberg, *Legends of the Jews* vol. 1, 54.

77. Nibley, "A New Look at the Pearl of Great Price," *Era*, July 1969, 106.

78. Cottle, *Liberty Jail and the Legacy of Joseph*, 30.

79. Nibley, "There Were Jaredites," *Era*, May 1956, 310.

80. Nibley, "A New Look at the Pearl of Great Price," *Era*, September 1969, 92.

81. Webb, *Smith as a Translator*, 140.

82. D&C 107:92.

83. Abraham 1:19.

84. Anderson, "The Book of the Revelation of Abraham," *Era* 1, 801.

85. JS-H 1:16.

86. Bruce R. McConkie, "The Three Pillars of Eternity," *BYU Devotional Address*, 17 February 1981.

87. Abraham 4:6-8, 15.

88. D&C 38:1.

89. Anderson, "The Book of the Revelation of Abraham," *Era* 1, 797-798; italics added.

90. 2 Corinthians 5:17.

Chapter 6: Facsimile No. 2

1. *BYU Studies* 17 (1977): 260.

2. Oliver Cowdery to Wm. Faye, Esq. *Messenger and Advocate*, December 1835, 236; italics added.

3. 2 Nephi 31:21.

4. 3 Nephi 11:31–32.

5. Facsimile No. 2, Explanation Fig. 3.

6. Ether 12:41.

7. Moroni 9:26.

8. Nibley, "I Have a Question," *Ensign*, March 1976, 34.

9. Michael Lyon, "Appreciating Hypocephali as Works of Art and Faith," Lecture from FARMS Book of Abraham Lecture Series, 24 March 1999, 2.

10. E. A. Wallis Budge, *The Mummy: A Handbook of Egyptian Funerary Archaeology,* 476–477.

11. Rhodes, "A Translation and Commentary of the Joseph Smith Hypocephalus," *BYU Studies* 17 no. 3 (1977): 259.

12. Rhodes, "A Translation and Commentary of the Joseph Smith Hypocephalus," *BYU Studies* 17 no. 3 (1977): 260.

13. Abraham 1:25–26.

14. Genesis 12:10; Abraham 3:15.

15. Genesis 37:2.

16. Abraham 3; Book of Exodus.

17. Lyon, "Appreciating Hypocephali as Works of Art and Faith," 10.

18. Budge, *The Gods of the Egyptians*, 1:131.

19. Budge, *The Gods of the Egyptians*, 1:163.

20. Abraham 1:25–26.

21. Lyon, "Appreciating Hypocephali as Works of Art and Faith."

22. Bruce R. McConkie, "Our Relationship with the Lord." *BYU Devotional Address*, 2 March 1982; italics added.

23. The October 1975 Relief Society Spiritual Living Lesson states that Jesus is the speaker delivering a message from the Father. *Relief Society Manual*, 1975.

24. Abraham 5:4.

25. Abraham 3:7, 18–21.

26. Abraham 1:16.

27. D&C 107:3.

28. Eliza R. Snow Smith, comp., *Biography and Family Records of Lorenzo Snow*, 46.

29. JD 6:4.

30. *BYU Studies* 17 (1977): 260.

31. "The Family: A Proclamation to the World," The Church of Jesus Christ of Latter-day Saints.

32. D&C 84:20–21.

33. CR, April 1921, 198.

34. D&C 132:20.

35. D&C 131:2.

36. Smith, "The King Follett Discourse 'A Newly Amalgamated Text,'" *BYU Studies* 18, no. 2 (1977): 201.

37. TPJS, 290.

38. Contained in the Explanation of Facsimile 2.

39. 1 Nephi 10:19.

40. John 14:20.

41. Rhodes, "A Translation and Commentary of the Joseph Smith Hypocephalus," *BYU Studies* 17 no. 3 (1977); Lyon, "Appreciating Hypocephali as Works of Art and Faith," 1, 3.

42. Pyramid Texts, e.g., Unas, line 558.

43. "Grammar and Alphabet of the Egyptian Language," second part, 1 degree. Transcript and copies of the original available in Special Collections, Harold B. Lee Library, Brigham Young University, as seen in Peterson, *The Story of the Book of Abraham*, 120.

44. Smith, "The King Follett Discourse 'A Newly Amalgamated Text,'" *BYU Studies* 18, no. 2 (1977): 202.

45. Mormon 9:9.

46. Smith, "The King Follett Discourse 'A Newly Amalgamated Text'" *BYU Studies* 18, no. 2 (1977): 202; "The King Follett Sermon," *Ensign*, May 1971, 17.

47. Cowdery, Oliver, *Messenger and Advocate*, December 1835, 236.

48. D&C 29:36.

49. Moses 4:3.

50. Hugh Nibley, "Hypocephalus Article," August 2, 1989, 7.

51. Lurker, Manfred, *An Illustrated Dictionary of the Gods and Symbols of Ancient Egypt*, 127.

52. Lurker, *An Illustrated Dictionary of the Gods and Symbols of Ancient Egypt*, 27.

53. D&C 121:36.

54. HC 4:536.

55. John 5:19.

56. Matthew 5:48 fn. b.

57. 3 Nephi 12:48.

58. 3 Nephi 27:27.

59. Bruce C. Hafen, *The Belonging Heart,* 315; italics added.

60. D&C 130:7.

61. Nibley, "Hypocephalus Article," 12.

62. Abraham 3:18-19.

63. McConkie, *Mormon Doctrine*, 28.

64. Rhodes, "A Translation and Commentary of the Joseph Smith Hypocephalus," *BYU Studies* 17 no. 3 (1977): 268, 270.

65. Joseph Smith, *Discourses of the Prophet Joseph Smith*, 56.

66. The Prophet Joseph's two great discourses, which are noted for knowledge concerning God, 7 April 1844 and 16 June 1844, used the word Eloheim as plural, meaning Gods or Council of Gods. At the turn of the century, it was clarified as Father when James Talmage, in his work *Jesus the Christ*, page 38, first stated, "Elohim, as understood and used in the restored Church of Jesus Christ, is the name-title of God the Eternal Father." The First Presidency and The Twelve, in their 30 June 1916 doctrinal exposition entitled "The Father and the Son," referenced Elder Talmage as to their usage of Elohim as Father.

67. Gordon T. Allred, *God the Father,* 18.

68. Smith, "The King Follett Discourse 'A Newly Amalgamated Text,'" *BYU Studies* 18, no. 2 (1977): 201.

69. Green, "New Light on Joseph Smith's Egyptian Papyri," *Era*, February 1968, 40.

70. Hugh Nibley, "What is 'The Book of Breathings'?" *BYU Studies* 11 no. 2 (1971): 173.

71. John 14:6.

72. 3 Nephi 27:13-14.

73. McConkie, *Mormon Doctrine*, 65.

74. Hebrews 9:12, 14-28.

75. Matthew 28:18.

76. Exodus 3:6.

77. Mormon 9:11.

78. 3 Nephi 15:5.

79. Ether 3:14.

80. John 8:58.

81. D&C 38:1.

82. D&C 76:40-42; 3 Nephi 27:13-14.

83. Abraham 1:18; 2:8-9.

84. John Taylor, *Items on Priesthood*, 31.

85. 1 John 1:5; reference the Topical Guide for other scriptures.

86. D&C 130:11; Revelation 3 & 4; Isaiah 62:2; 65:15; Mosiah 5:9-14; 3 Nephi 20:39.

87. 3rd Enoch 26:4-5, 7, and 8. Charlesworth, *The Old Testament Pseudepigrapha* vol. 1, 280-281.

88. Budge, *The Mummy: A Handbook of Egyptian Funerary Archaeology*, 318.

89. D&C 84:98-102; Psalms 96:1; Revelation 15:3; Alma 5:26.

90. Budge, *The Mummy: A Handbook of Egyptian Funerary Archaeology*, 316.

91. JST Genesis 14:30-31.

92. Galatians 3:26-29.

93. 3 Nephi 15:9.

94. 2 Nephi 32:5.

95. 1 Nephi 10:19.

96. Anderson, "The Book of The Revelation of Abraham" *Era* 1, 713.

97. B. H. Roberts, *The Gospel and Man's Relationship to Deity*, 189.

98. Parley P. Pratt, *Key to the Science of Theology,* 40.

99.   Roberts, *The Gospel and Man's Relationship to Deity*, 193–194.

100. D&C 130:22.

101. Smith, "The King Follett Discourse 'A Newly Amalgamated Text,'" *BYU Studies* 18, no. 2 (1977): 204.

102. Talmage, James E., *The Articles of Faith*, 168.

103. Anderson, "The Book of the Revelation of Abraham," *Era* 1, 793.

104. Galatians 5:22–23.

105. D&C 121:46.

106. D&C 88:13.

107. TPJS, 149–150.

108. Budge, *The Gods of the Egyptians*, 1:437.

109. Moses 4:26; italics added.

110. Lurker, *Illustrated Dictionary of the Gods and Symbols of Ancient Egypt*, 59.

111. Budge, *The Gods of the Egyptians*, 1:437.

112. Nibley, *Abraham in Egypt*, 120–121.

113. Budge, *The Gods of the Egyptians*, 1:434.

114. Rhodes, "A Translation and Commentary of the Joseph Smith Hypocephalus," *BYU Studies* 17 no. 3 (1977): 272.

115. Revelation 7:2–3.

116. D&C 77:8.

117. 3 Nephi 16:5.

118. Moses 7:62.

119. Rhodes, "A Translation and Commentary of the Joseph Smith Hypocephalus," *BYU Studies* 17 no. 3 (1977): 273.

120. Lundwall, *Temples of the Most High*, 144.

121. HC 5:389.

122. McKay, David O., 17 January 1955 address given at Pesega, Samoa. Microfilm reel 15, in LDS Archives.

123. D&C 35:19.

124. D&C 27:5, 12-13; HC 3:385, 387; Joseph Fielding Smith, *The Way to Perfection*, 288; Alvin Dyer, *The Refiner's Fire*, 180-183.

125. Gaster, "Memoirs of the Patriarchs," in *The Dead Sea Scriptures*, 433.

126. 3 Nephi 12:48 fn. a.

127. Matthew 5:48 fn. b.

128. Jacob 1:19.

129. Moses 8:15.

130. Nibley, "A New Look at the Pearl of Great Price," *Era*, April 1969, 72.

131. Webb, *Smith as a Translator*, 159.

132. Deuteronomy 29:29.

133. Pratt, "Spiritual Communication," in Lundwall, *Temples of the Most High*, 145.

134. Nibley, "A New Look at the Pearl of Great Price," *Era*, March 1969, 80.

135. Abraham 3:23, as seen in Hugh Nibley, "The Early Christian Prayer Circle", *BYU Studies* 19, no. 1 (1978): 64.

136. 1 Nephi 10:19.

137. Pratt, "Spiritual Communication," in Lundwall, *Temples of the Most High*, 145.

138. "The Family, A Proclamation to the World."

139. Lurker, *An Illustrated Dictionary of the Gods and Symbols of Ancient Egypt*, 100.

140. Smith, "The King Follett Discourse 'A Newly Amalgamated Text,'" *BYU Studies* 18, no. 2 (1977): 205-206.

141. JST Exodus 34:1.

142. JS-H 1:17.

143. The King Follett Discourse given April 7, 1844, and the Discourse in the Grove, east of the temple, just eight days before his death.

Chapter 7: Facsimile No. 3

1. Gee, *A History of the Joseph Smith Papyri and Book of Abraham,* 5; and see Gee's appendix "The Joseph Smith Papyri: Then and Now," about the Scroll of Hor.

2. 1 Peter 1:2.

3. Helck, Rituliszenen ... Rameses' II., 74, as seen in Nibley, "What is 'The Book of Breathings'?" *BYU Studies* 11, no. 2 (1971): 182.

4. D&C 109:77.

5. D&C 76:56.

6. D&C 132:29.

7. Alma 5:24.

8. D&C 132:31.

9. D&C 132:37, and compare TPJS, 150-151, 322-323.

10. Bruce R. McConkie, *Doctrinal New Testament Commentary* vol. 3, 329.

11. Hugh Nibley, "I Have a Question," *Ensign*, March 1976, 36.

12. *Hymns*, The Church of Jesus Christ of Latter-day Saints, 250.

13. John 17.

14. John 14:10-12, 17, and 20-21.

15. D&C 132:37.

16. Pratt, *Key to the Science of Theology*, 61.

17. D&C 132:49.

18. Revelation 7:13-15.

19. D&C 132:20.

20. D&C 132:20 & 37.

21. 2 Peter 1:10-11.

22. TPJS, 64.

23. TPJS, 237.

24. *Era*, June 1970, 65-66.

25. Ezra T. Benson, *Ensign*, October 1986, 5; August 1985, 10; *BYU Devotional Address*, April 12, 1977. Marion G. Romney, *Era*, November 1949, 719; December 1965, 1115; *Ensign*, July 1972, 98. Bruce R. McConkie, *BYU Devotional Address*, October 11, 1966; March 25, 1969; *Era*, December 1969, 84; *Ensign*, January 1974, 45; November 1977, 33; *The Promised Messiah*, 575.

26. Moroni 10:31-34.

27. CR, April 1921, 198.

28. Philippians 2:15.

29. D&C 132:30.

30. *Era*, May 1965, 310.

31. JD 15:299.

32. Revelation 3:21.

33. The three goals of the Church were given by President
     Spencer W. Kimball at the October 1981 General
     Conference. They are (1) To proclaim the gospel to the world
     in order to bring God's children to the ordinances of the
     temple. (2) To perfect the Saints through the ordinances of
     the House of the Lord. (3) To redeem the dead through the
     vicarious ordinances of the temple.

34. D&C 132:19.

35. D&C 84:34.

36. Daniel Tyler, *Juvenile Instructor*, May 15, 1880, 111.

37. Helaman 10:4-7.

38. D&C 76:50-70; 94-96.

39. TPJS, 303.

40. Orson Pratt, *The Seer*, 297.

41. D&C 132:6, 20.

42. D&C 121:45-46.

43. Each eternity has a period of accomplishment, completion,
     or fulfillment. William W. Phelps, David Hyrum Smith, and
     Bruce R. McConkie, at various times, expressed that the
     length of an eternity is 2,555,000,000 years. With the Book
     of Abraham as one's source, beginning with the statement that
     "One day in Kolob is equal to a thousand years according to
     the measurement of this earth, "we need only multiply 1000
     by 365 days of the year, times 7000 (the temporal portion of
     the earth's existence) to arrive at the number of 2,555,000,000.
     It is interesting that a secular discovery in 1999, having to do
     with shale in Australia, has altered the scientific community's
     theory about the age of the earth. With this recent finding, the
     earth's age of existence is now purported to be 2,700,000,000
     years old. This is surprisingly close to information revealed first
     to father Abraham and through the Book of Abraham to the
     Prophet Joseph Smith as he translated it.

44. Nibley, "There Were Jaredites," *Era*, May 1956, 310.

45. Hugh Nibley, "The Stick of Judah," *Era*, February 1953, 124.

46. D&C 85:8; Jasher 77:42-47.

47. Revelation 3:21.

48. TPJS, 64.

49. D&C 107:18-19.

50. See Endnote 9.

51. Nibley, *Abraham in Egypt*, 430.

52. Nibley, *Abraham in Egypt*, 444.

53. Nibley, "There Were Jaredites," 310.

54. Nibley, "I Have a Question," Ensign, March 1976, 36.

55. Era, April, 1956, 252.

56. Abraham 3:23.

57. Abraham 1:2.

58. The Academic Review 'B.Y. Academy,' 1 no. 6, March 1885, 46, as seen in Walter L. Whipple, "The St. Louis Museum of the 1850's and the Two Egyptian Mummies and Papyri," *BYU Studies* 10, no. 1 (1970): 63-64.

59. Matthew 18:23.

60. D&C 84:36-38.

61. Acts 16:17; D&C 84:36.

62. Hyrum L. Andrus, *Principles of Perfection*, 329.

Chapter 8: Conclusion

1. Moses 6:61-62.

2. Taylor, *The Gospel Kingdom*, 1.

3. HC 6:78.

4. Pratt, "Spiritual Communication," in Lundwall, *Temples of the Most High*, 144.

5. Gaster, "The Last Jubilee: A Sermon," in *The Dead Sea Scriptures*, 433–434.

6. D&C 8:11.

7. TPJS, 364.

8. JD 4:5.

9. Bruce R. McConkie, *Ensign*, November 1978, 61.

10. 1 Thessalonians 5:21.

11. D&C 76:7.

12. Alma 32:35.

13. Smith, "The King Follett Sermon," *Ensign*, May 1971, 14.

14. Spencer W. Kimball, *Abraham: An Example to Fathers*, 8.

15. D&C 132:32.

16. Moses 6:35–36.

17. Revelation 2:11, 17; 3:6, 13.

18. Nibley, "I Have a Question," *Ensign*, March 1976, 36.

Appendix A: Melchizedek and Shem

1. Cottle, chapter 3, "Joseph's Legacy of Scriptures" in Liberty Jail and the Legacy of Joseph.

2. D&C 76:57.

3. Taylor, John, *Times and Seasons* Vol. 5, 746, as found in Lundwall, *A Compilation Containing the Lectures on Faith*, 93; John A. Widtsoe, *Evidences and Reconciliations* 3 Vols., 232; Alvin R. Dyer, *Who Am I?*, 400. For the oft quoted problem of D&C 84:14 see Alma E. Gygi, "I Have a Question," *Ensign*, November 1973, 15.

4. Dyer, *The Lord Speaketh*, 285-286. This was written six years after Bruce R. McConkie wrote his concerns about there being two generations between Melchizedek and Shem. See McConkie, *Mormon Doctrine*, 431-432.

5. D&C 107:2; 138:41.

6. Alma 13:17-18; Gygi, "I Have a Question," *Ensign*, November 1973, 15.

7. Ginsberg, *Legends of the Jews* vol. 1, 233.

8. Jasher, 6:11.

Appendix D: Two Equal Powers and Capacities

1. Kabbalah, chapter 8:219 & 222. Kabbalah are sacred Jewish writings.

2. See Esther chapter 1.

3. "The Family: A Proclamation to the World."

4. D&C 132:59.

5. D&C 132:63.

Appendix E: Four Angels--Sons of God

1. Revelation 7:2-3.

2. TPJS, 321.

3. CR, April 1929, 110.

4. CR, April 1992, 94.

Appendix F: An Eternity

1. James R. Harris, "Eternal Progression and the Foreknowledge of God," *BYU Studies* 8, no. 1 (1967): 37.

2.   Mosiah 3:5; D&C 76:4; Lundwall, *Temples of the Most High*, 266.

3.   Isaiah 66:22.

4.   2 Peter 3:13; Revelation 21:1.

5.   D&C 76:4; Mosiah 3:5 fn. d.

6.   W.W. Phelps, *Times and Seasons* 5:758; David Hyrum Smith, Diary 15 July 1853 to 4 June 1864 Library-Archives The Reorganized Church of Jesus Christ of Latter-day Saints, Independence, Missouri; Bruce R. McConkie, "Seven Deadly Heresies," *1980 Devotional Speeches of the Year*, 75; Bruce R. McConkie, *The Mortal Messiah: From Bethlehem to Calvary* Book 1, 29.

7.   Book of Abraham, Facsimile 2, Explanation Fig. 1.

8.   USA Today, 14 August 1999, 1.

9.   Moses 1:39.

10. Orson Pratt, *Wonders of the Universe*, 209; JD 17:332.

Appendix G: Bible and Civilization Chronology

1.   Scott, *Voices from the Dust*, 9.

2.   Scott, *Voices from the Dust*, 11.

3.   Widtsoe, *Evidences and Reconciliations*, 127.

4.   Scott, *Voices from the Dust*, 11.

5.   James Mellaart, *The Beginning of Village and Urban Life*, 620, as seen in Nibley, *Old Testament and Related Studies* vol. 1, 31.

6.   Scott, *Voices from the Dust*, 11.

7.   Nibley, *Old Testament and Related Studies* vol. 1, 33.

8.   Helaman 8:18

Bibliography

Alcuin, Albinus, trans. *The Book of Jasher*. New York: M.M. Noah & A.S. Gould, 1840; cited as Jasher.

Allred, Gordon T. *God the Father*. Salt Lake City: Bookcraft, n.d.

Andrus, Hyrum L. *Principles of Perfection*. Salt Lake City: Bookcraft, 1970.

Bible Lands Posters Commentary. Salt Lake City: The Church of Jesus Christ of Latter-day Saints, 1986.

Brigham Young University (BYU) Devotional Address. Provo, UT: Brigham Young University, October 11, 1966; March 25, 1969; April 12, 1977; 17 February 1981; 2 March 1982.

Brigham Young University (BYU) Studies. Provo, Utah: Brigham Young University, 1959 – .

Budge, E. A. Wallis. *The Gods of the Egyptians, Vol. 1 & 2*. New York: Dover Publication, Inc., 1969.

---. *The Mummy: A Handbook of Egyptian Funerary Archaeology*. New York: Dover Publication, Inc., 1989.

Cannon, George Q. *Gospel Truth*. Compiled by Jerreld L. Newquist. Salt Lake City: Deseret Book, 1974.

Charlesworth, James H, ed. *The Old Testament Pseudepigrapha, Apocalyptic Literatures and Testaments* vol. 1 & 2. Garden City, New York: Doubleday, 1985.

Conference Report. Salt Lake City: The Church of Jesus Christ of Latter-day Saints, 1880 – ; cited as CR.

Cottle, Thomas D., and Patricia C. Cottle. *Liberty Jail and the Legacy of Joseph*. Portland, OR: Insight, 1998.

Dyer, Alvin R. *The Lord Speaketh*. Salt Lake City: Deseret Book, 1964.

---. *The Refiner's Fire*. Salt lake City: Deseret Book Company, 1980.

---. *Who Am I?* Salt Lake City: Deseret Book, 1968.

Earth's Mysterious Places. Pleasantville, NY: The Reader's Digest Association, Inc., 1992.

Encyclopedia of Mormonism. Selected by Daniel H. Ludlow, S. Kent Brown, and John W. Welch. New York: Macmillan Publishing Company, 1992.

Ensign. Salt Lake City: The Church of Jesus Christ of Latter-day Saints, 1971 –.

"The Family: A Proclamation to the World." Salt Lake City: The Church of Jesus Christ of Latter-day Saints, 1995.

Gaster, Theodor H. *The Dead Sea Scriptures*. Garden City, NY: Anchor Press/Doubleday, 1976.

Gee, John A. *A History of the Joseph Smith Papyri and Book of Abraham*. Provo, UT: Foundation for Ancient Research and Mormon Studies (FARMS), 1999.

Ginsberg, Louis. *Legends of the Jews* vol. 1. The Jewish Publication Society of America, Philadelphia, 1921.

Hafen, Bruce C. and Marie K. Hafen. *The Belonging Heart*. Salt Lake City: Deseret Book, n.d.

Hymns. Salt Lake City: The Church of Jesus Christ of Latter-day Saints, 1979.

Improvement Era. Salt Lake City, 1897-1970; cited as Era.

Journal of Discourses 26 vols. London: Latter-day Saints' Book Deport, 1854-86; cited as JD.

The Juvenile Instructor. Salt Lake City, 1866-1930.

Kimball, Spencer W. *Abraham: An Example to Father*. Salt Lake City: Deseret Book, 1977.

Lundwall, N.B., comp. *A Compilation Containing the Lectures on Faith*. Salt Lake City: Bookcraft, n.d.

---. *Temples of the Most High*. Salt Lake City: Bookcraft, 1949.

Lurker, Manfred. *An Illustrated Dictionary of the Gods and Symbols of Ancient Egypt*. London: Thames and Hudson Ltd., 1982.

Lyon, Michael. "Appreciating Hypocephali as Works of Art and Faith." Lecture from Foundation for Ancient Research and Mormon Studies (FARMS) Book of Abraham Lecture Series, 24 March 1999.

McConkie, Bruce R. *Doctrinal New Testament Commentary* vol. 3. Salt Lake City: Bookcraft, 1973.

---. *Mormon Doctrine*. Salt Lake City: Bookcraft, 1958.

---. *The Mortal Messiah: From Bethlehem to Calvary* Book 1. Salt Lake City: Deseret Book, 1981.

---. *The Promised Messiah*. Salt Lake City: Deseret Book, 1978.

---. "Seven Deadly Heresies." *1980 Devotional Speeches of the Year.* Provo, UT: Brigham Young University Press, 1981.

McKay, David O. 17 January 1955 address given at Pesega, Samoa. Microfilm reel 15, in LDS Archives.

Melchizedek Priesthood Manual. Salt Lake City: The Church of Jesus Christ of Latter-day Saints, 1973-74.

Messenger and Advocate. Kirtland, Ohio, 1834-37.

Nibley, Hugh. *Abraham in Egypt*. Salt Lake City: Deseret Book Company, 1981.

---. "Hypocephalus Article." August 2, 1989, unpublished, in possession of author.

---. *Old Testament and Related Studies* vol. 1. Salt Lake City: Deseret Book, 1986.

Packer, Boyd K. *The Holy Temple*. Salt Lake City: Bookcraft, 1980.

Peterson, H. Donl. *The Story of the Book of Abraham*. Salt Lake City: Deseret Book, 1995.

Pratt, Orson *The Seer*. Orem, UT: Grandin Book Co., 1994.

---. *Wonders of the Universe*. Salt Lake City: Nels B. Lundwall, 1937.

Pratt, Parley P. *Key to the Science of Theology*. Salt Lake City: Deseret News Steam Printing Establishment, 1874.

Relief Society Manual. Salt Lake City: The Church of Jesus Christ of Latter-day Saints, 1975.

Ricks, Stephen D., Donald W. Parry, and Andrew H. Hedges, ed. "Eyewitness, Hearsay, and Physical Evidence of the Joseph Smith Papyri." *The Disciple as Witness*. Foundation for Ancient Research and Mormon Studies (FARMS), Provo, UT, 2000.

Roberts, B. H. *The Gospel and Man's Relationship to Deity*. Salt Lake City: Deseret Book, n.d.

Scott, Glenn A. *Voices from the Dust: New Light on an Ancient American Record*. Independence, MO: School of Saints, 1996.

Skousen, W. Cleon. *The First 2,000 Years*. Salt Lake City: Bookcraft, 1953.

Smith, David Hyrum. Diary 15 July 1853 to 4 June 1864. Library-Archives, The Reorganized Church of Jesus Christ of Latter-day Saints (RLDS), Independence, Missouri.

Smith, Eliza R. Snow, comp. *Biography and Family Records of Lorenzo Snow*. Salt Lake City: Deseret News Company, 1884.

Smith, Joseph F. *Gospel Doctrine*. Salt Lake City: Deseret Book, 1939.

Smith, Joseph Fielding. *The Way to Perfection*. Salt Lake City: Deseret Book Co., 1984.

Smith, Joseph Jr. *Discourses of the Prophet Joseph Smith*. Salt Lake City: Deseret Book Co., 1977.

---. *History of The Church of Jesus Christ of Latter-day Saints*. Salt Lake City: Deseret Book, 1976; cited as HC.

---. *Teachings of the Prophet Joseph Smith*. Compiled by Joseph Fielding Smith. Salt Lake City: Deseret Book, 1976; cited as TPJS.

---. *The Words of Joseph Smith*. Compiled by Andrew F. Ehat and Lyndon W. Cook. Provo, UT: Religious Studies Center, 1980; cited as WJS.

Talmage, James E. *The Articles of Faith*. Salt Lake City: The Deseret News, 1901.

---. *Jesus the Christ*. Salt Lake City: Deseret Book, 1977.

Taylor, John. *The Gospel Kingdom*. Salt Lake City: Bookcraft, 1943.

---. *Items on Priesthood*. Salt Lake City: Deseret Book, n.d.

Times and Seasons. Nauvoo, Illinois, 1839-46.

Todd, Jay M. *The Saga of the Book of Abraham*. Salt Lake City: Deseret Book, 1969.

USA Today. Mclean, VA: Gannett Co., Inc. 14 August 1999.

Ware, Richard. "The Holy Priesthood, A History and Doctrine of the Priesthood as Taught by Joseph Smith and his Successors and as Conatined in the Latter-day Saint Scripture." Rosetta Research Group, 1996, in author's possession.

Webb, Robert C. *Smith as a Translator*. Salt Lake City: Deseret News Press, 1936.

Whiston, William, trans. *The Works of Flavius Josephus*. Cincinnati: A. M. E. Morgan and Co, 1847.

Widtsoe, John A. *Evidences and Reconciliations*. Arranged by G. Homer Durham. Salt Lake City: Bookcraft, 1960.

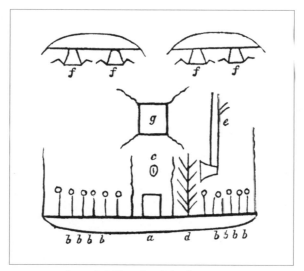

Sacred Ojibwa birch bark writings

a. Door of Temple Wigwam
b. Twelve Wise Men
c. Great Stone
d. Tree of Life
e. Pipe of Power
f. Four Great Spirits "which looked down on the earth"
g. Four Sacred Directions around Hole (navel) of the Earth

Kohl, Johann Georg, Kitchi-Gami, Minnesota Historical Society Press, St. Paul, MN, 1885 pp. 151, 215, 403-404

About the Author

Thomas D. Cottle graduated from Utah State University (BS) and Marquette University School of Dentistry (DDS). He is a veteran of the Korean war, serving in the United States Air Force. He has served as a bishop, stake president and a counselor in the first Portland Oregon Temple presidency. He and his wife, Mary Lou (deceased), served as missionaries in the Minnesota, Minneapolis Mission. They have eight children.

He married Patricia, the mother of four, in 1994. They have served as missionaries in the Missouri, Independence and Ukraine, Kiev Missions. Currently, they are laboring in the Zimbabwe, Harare Mission. They are the authors of *Liberty Jail and the Legacy of Joseph*.